How to Get the Most Out of Philosophy

SIXTH EDITION

DOUGLAS J. SOCCIO

THOMSON

WADSWORTH

Australia • Canada • Mexico • Singapore • Spain
United Kingdom • United States

How to Get the Most Out of
Philosophy, Sixth Edition
Douglas J. Soccio

Publisher/Executive Editor: Holly J. Allen
Acquisitions Editor: Steve Wainwright
Assistant Editors: Lee McCracken and Barbara Hillaker
Editorial Assistant: Gina Kessler
Technology Project Manager: Julie Aguilar
Marketing Manager: Worth Hawes
Marketing Assistant: Alexandra Tran
Project Manager, Editorial Production: Megan E. Hansen

Creative Director: Rob Hugel
Executive Art Director: Maria Epes
Print Buyer: Linda Hsu
Permissions Editor: Roberta Broyer
Production Service: Mona Tiwary, International Typesetting and Composition
Copy Editor: Saloni Narang
Cover Designer: Yvo Riezebos
Compositor: International Typesetting and Composition
Printer: Thomson West

Thomson Higher Education
10 Davis Drive
Belmont, CA 94002-3098
USA

For more information about our products, contact us at:
Thomson Learning Academic Resource Center
1-800-423-0563

For permission to use material from this text or product, submit a request online at
http://www.thomsonrights.com.
Any additional questions about permissions can be submitted by e-mail to
thomsonrights@thomson.com.

Library of Congress Control Number: 2006924671

Student Edition: ISBN 0-495-17223-5

For students everywhere—
but especially for first-generation students
and their families

This is your education. Customize it. Work at it. By enrolling in college, you are accepting a personal invitation to participate in a "great conversation." Plato characterized his teacher, the philosopher Socrates, as a guide who helped others climb out of the cave of ignorance. But Socrates, one of the greatest teachers of all time, always insisted that the teacher only "draws wisdom" out of the pupil—and only the pupil can provide the will.

In the spirit of Socrates, I hope this book helps you on your own journey "out of the cave."

Contents

Preface to Instructors (and Curious Students)

It is easy to assume that students know more about making their ways through college than many of them do. Things that seem obvious to professors aren't always obvious to students. Things like actually studying the course syllabus—and keeping it for the entire term. Things like carefully following formatting instructions for writing assignments. Things like taking textbooks to class. Things like using the glossary and index. Things like dropping by during scheduled office hours and asking questions.

When the first edition of *How to Get the Most Out of Philosophy* came out bundled with *Archetypes of Wisdom*, it generated two equally intense reactions. On the positive side, it was immensely popular. I was surprised and gratified by how many instructors and students requested additional, stand-alone copies, which, unfortunately, were not available at that time.

Alas, that first edition also provoked a reaction from instructors (not students) who snidely trivialized *How to Get the Most Out of Philosophy* as "hokey," "simplistic," and "belaboring the obvious." I assumed then, as I do now, that some of these disdainful instructors teach at colleges whose undergraduates arrive having just completed four years of sophisticated college prep courses in high school. But even if some or most of *How to Get the Most Out of Philosophy* is obvious to this fortunate student cohort, it is not obvious to most students. I also suspect that some of the most disdainful instructors were themselves good students who are simply unaware of the sorts of things many promising students simply haven't learned in high school or at home, things that it's pretty easy to assume someone else has covered.

But the increasing success of each subsequent edition of *How to Get the Most Out of Philosophy* confirms my conviction that, today more than ever, most students begin college ignorant of at least some of the practices, expectations, and cultural norms that are essential for getting a good education—and that seem so "obvious" once they're expressed and internalized.

The usefulness of this little book is attested to by the many students and philosophy professors who recommend it as a "handbook of student wisdom" to friends, relatives, and counselors—and not just to philosophy students and philosophy teachers.

As college becomes accessible to more people, today's diverse student body will include ever-increasing numbers of first-generation students; students trying to juggle family responsibilities, jobs, and solid course loads; students from shaky environments; and students who did "well enough" in high school, but still arrive in college a bit naive, disorganized, marginally motivated, and, unsurprisingly, even a little insecure. *How to Get the Most Out of Philosophy* is for these students especially and for the instructors who want to help them succeed, not just in class, but also in college and beyond.

A LESSON LEARNED THE HARD WAY: A PERSONAL NOTE TO PHILOSOPHY STUDENTS AND TEACHERS

As a first-generation college student, I know firsthand the consequences of "not knowing the ropes." When I was in high school, my teachers and family just assumed that I'd probably go to college—so I just assumed it, too. Lacking any more precise goal than "going to college" as cheaply as possible, I began my college education by driving across town to the closest community college. I never thought one way or the other about the long-term effects of going to a community college as opposed to a big-name college or university. I just had the vague notion that some people "went to college" and then went out and asked for—and got—jobs. As far as I was concerned, people who "went to college" were "successful." All of this was very general, however, and so I naturally selected a "general education" major.

When it came time to transfer to the cross-town state university, I approached a couple of my favorite community college instructors for letters of recommendation. I figured that my instructors would be happy to recommend me to a four-year college because I got good grades in their courses and because I liked them and they seemed to like me. It wasn't that simple. My professors politely informed me that they knew nothing about me. I had never been by their offices, and I had taken only one course from each of them. Eventually, they took pity on me. After checking my transcript and chatting with me about my plans, my instructors wrote me generic letters of recommendation.

In hindsight, I can see that I brought a certain working-class ethic with me to college. One tenet of this ethic is that an upright person does not use flattery to get ahead because you are expected to stand or fall on the quality of your work. Based on my understanding of that don't-be-a-flatterer principle, I treated asking my teachers for help outside of class and talking with them about their classes as flattery. I was so worried about being perceived as a flatterer, although that's not the word I used then, that I missed out on one of the real joys of going to college.

Although I had plenty of love and encouragement from my family, I had no one to teach me about letters of recommendation or how to relate to a "Professor." My family and I knew that going to college was important, but none of us knew the ropes, as they say.

My point here is not to tell stories about myself, but to suggest how easy it is to lose sight of the complexity of the day-to-day factors that bear on student success or failure. The philosophy instructors who reacted negatively to the first edition of *How to Get the Most Out of Philosophy* may have focused so much attention on the subject matter at hand that they overlooked some of these complicating life factors. The fact is, however, that the great variety of students going to college today only intensifies the need for books like this one.

Today, college professors cannot assume that their students have graduated from high school with solid reading, writing, and thinking skills. In some parts of the country, it is still possible to graduate from high school without ever writing an argument paper or analytic essay. As a consequence, beginning philosophy students may have limited experience with the kinds of reading and writing that their philosophy courses will require. Just because students have done something called "critical thinking," this doesn't guarantee that they've been exposed to critical thinking as philosophers understand that term. There is a good chance that your philosophy course is the first sustained exposure to thinking and writing critically about critical literature that some of your students have ever had.

Like its predecessors, the sixth edition of *How to Get the Most Out of Philosophy* is predicated on the modest notion that sometimes just the right word of advice or encouragement can make a difference between success and failure. We can all benefit, now and again, from the kind of guidance and encouragement that are easy to overlook or trivialize. Take it from a fellow for whom the obvious wasn't all that obvious when he needed it most: Belaboring the obvious can be a labor of love.

NEW TO THE SIXTH EDITION

Users of previous editions of *How to Get the Most Out of Philosophy* will note that this Sixth Edition has been rearranged as a "study guide of study guides." To that end, I have trimmed some repetitions and rearranged and combined chapters and sections into self-contained mini study guides within a larger (but not large) philosophically oriented study guide. In that spirit:

- The student-praised chapter, "Student Wisdom," has been moved forward and recast as two chapters—Chapter 1: Student Wisdom: Getting the Most Out of Yourself and Chapter 2: Changing What You Can.

- "Relating to Your Professor" is now part of Chapter 4: How to Thrive in a Philosophy Class.

- Guidelines for reading philosophy have been combined with a broader discussion of what it means to read critically, combining what previously were two chapters into one chapter.

- The style guide and tips and advice about tests and letters of recommendation are provided as Appendix A: Simplified Style Guide for Excellent Papers, Appendix B: Test Taking, and Appendix C: Letters of Recommendation.

- Selected data from the most recent National Survey of Student Engagement are used throughout the text to provide students with a sense of what has been found to work—and not work—in such real life areas as plagiarism, communicating with professors, and allocating time for studying.
- The "Beginning Philosopher's Bibliography" and the list of online sources have been updated.

SOCCIO ON THE WORLD WIDE WEB

The *Wadsworth Philosophy Home* is a nifty website provided by the publisher of this book. The *Wadsworth Philosophy Home* has all sorts of information about Wadsworth publications (as you might expect). What you might not expect, however, is that many of their authors, who are practicing philosophers with differing interests and styles, post interesting information there, too. This website is a great opportunity to browse in a specialized "virtual bookstore" and to learn from philosophers from around the world.

For additional links and learning resources go to the Wadsworth philosophy home website:

http://www.thomsonedu.com/philosophy

Introduction

What to Expect

> If we do only what is required of us we are
> slaves, the moment we do more we are free.
> CICERO

How to Get the Most Out of Philosophy, Sixth Edition, can help you get the most out of more than just your philosophy courses—it can also help you get the most out of yourself. Much of *How to Get the Most Out of Philosophy* is based on articles and books about teaching, on conversations with professors at community colleges, private liberal arts colleges, state universities, and world-famous research universities. But most of all, it is based on my experiences with thousands of students of almost every conceivable background and ability.

Some of what follows will probably be new to you, and some of it will almost certainly be the same old stuff you've heard most of your student life. That's okay. The point of hearing certain things again is edification, a process that strengthens our good qualities and changes us for the better. Because it's so easy to get caught up in the moment or bogged down and confused, it helps to be encouraged by being reminded of how much we already know.

The explanations and examples in *How to Get the Most Out of Philosophy* are deliberately brief. That way you can scan the entire book quickly, and then concentrate on pertinent sections as often as you need to. Everything that follows has been chosen to help you study efficiently. More than that, this is a compendium of the accumulated wisdom that scores of philosophy students and instructors have developed to cope with unnecessary anxiety, to get satisfactory grades and to learn something of value.

You can read *How to Get the Most Out of Philosophy* relatively quickly, and I highly recommend reading it straight through right away. Doing so will get you fired up about your education, about yourself, and about philosophy.

Succeeding in a philosophy class requires a willingness to think in a structured, critical way at scheduled times, whether or not you are in a pondering mood—just like being a member of the soccer team requires you to practice or play at scheduled times, whether or not you are in the "soccering" mood. Your coach may put you in as the goalie when you would prefer to play forward—just like your philosophy instructor may want you to think and write about the existence of God when you would rather think and write about the pursuit of pleasure.

Probably the most persistent—and false—form of student self-sabotage is the notion that you need to be "in the mood" to think carefully and to study diligently. As a matter of fact, thinking and studying are more like exercising and eating wisely than we sometimes want to admit. Most of us have the ability to think carefully—just like we have the ability to exercise or eat wisely—whether or not we are in the mood.

You might be thinking, "Okay, that sounds great. But in the real world I have to deal with boring teachers and uninteresting textbooks. And that makes studying and participating hard." So what? (I ask gently.) College ought to be difficult sometimes, just like friendship and work. Besides, even if you can't do anything directly about the subject matter itself, about your teacher, or about which text your teacher assigns, you can exert considerable influence on how you deal with each of them. What you do—and how you do it—will almost certainly influence your instructor. But whether it does or not, you are always better off to do your part.

So why not give yourself every advantage and begin every class with a firm resolve to participate, to get the most out of philosophy and out of college by getting the most out of yourself whether or not you are "in the mood"?

1

Student Wisdom: Getting the Most Out of Yourself

> Would a sick person be helped
> Merely by reading a medical text?
> SHANTIVEDA

You already possess most of the skills and abilities necessary to succeed in a philosophy class because you already possess many of the traits needed to succeed at other things. Consider how much time sports fans put into *studying* sports; how much time and energy people put into *learning about* their mp3 players, blogs, cars, favorite bands; how much they put into *practicing* basketball, soccer, video games. Consider how much money we spend on hobbies and amusement. In other words, consider just how much sweat, work, energy, and sacrifice we are willing to make for things we care about or want to be good at. Notice how easy it is to remember the date and starting time of the big game or concert—even if it's weeks away.

These are the same habits and skills—repetition, regular practice, and paying attention—that make successful students more successful. In other words, as you may already know, we get good at what we work at and we work at what interests us. What you may not know, however, is that the relation between interest and practice goes both ways. We also grow interested in what we practice. Not always, of course, especially if we feel coerced into doing something, but often enough to teach us something valuable about college and about life. We have more control than we realize—or always want.

This chapter is a summary of good, field-tested advice that I think of as student wisdom. Combining new information and ways of looking at things with reminders of what you already know about school success is a great way to strengthen your commitment to your college education and inspire you when the going gets rough.

> The most valuable result of all education is to make you do the thing you have to do, when it ought to be done, whether you like it or not.—Thomas Huxley

WHAT AM I DOING HERE?

Here is a surprisingly valuable philosophical exercise to get you started, especially if you feel like you're only going to college because you "have to." First, note that feeling like you have to go to college is no permanent obstacle because you can do well at things that you don't particularly want to do, if for no other reason than as a matter of pride—self-respect. On the other hand, sometimes, we need psychological motivation to shore us up. This is where writing down your reasons, your own honest, true, unadulterated reasons, for going to college comes in. Just thinking or talking about them is not as insightful as writing them out—no matter how hokey that may seem. And let's be clear from the start. If you're losing steam or never had it to begin with, you're probably not the best person to decide what's hokey and what's not.

If you decide to give this exercise a try, do so right now, before reading any further. Once you've made your list, keep it. Be sure to write down all the reasons you have for going to college. List your real reasons, not your public, face-saving, ought-to-be reasons, but your honest, genuine reasons. You're not doing this exercise for other people; you are doing it for yourself. This is an exercise in Socratic insight, a step toward knowing yourself a little better. If your main reason for going to college is because you need a degree to get a certain kind of job, say so. On the other hand, if you're going to college to put off getting a "real job," say so. If you're going to college because you want to broaden yourself, say so; if you're going because you don't know what else to do at this stage of your life, say that.

List as many reasons as you have. Don't worry if your reasons appear to be inconsistent or even silly. Almost any reason for going to college can become a good reason, if it isn't already.

Once you've made your list, take some time to analyze it. If you're like lots of students, you have many reasons for being in college, including a general desire to learn, a desire for the social prestige attached to being a college graduate coupled with a fear of not having a college degree, and the expectation that a college degree will lead to a financially comfortable and personally rewarding career.

■ **Whatever's on your list, and whatever your current circumstances, remember that you have decided that going to college is better than all of the alternatives.** When you get discouraged, remind yourself that you are where you have decided it's best to be at the moment. Reread your list whenever you wonder: "Why am I doing this?" Remind yourself that you have your reasons and that they are good ones. Update your list as you discover additional reasons for going to college.

■ **Regularly reassess your goals.** An academic or vocational degree requires a significant investment of time, effort, and money. Failure to identify your own clear reasons for going to college can result in wasting all three. At the same time, a big part of getting an education is the sort of ongoing self-discovery that can result in new goals. So don't be discouraged if your plans change two or three times during your college career. The crucial thing is to be as clear as you can about your real goals. No one else's opinions about going to college can give you the energy and commitment required for college success.

■ **It's all right if this is not the time for you to be in college.** You're the only one who can get deep enough into your motives and resources to know what's right for you now. If you are not ready to concentrate and sacrifice, or if you have too many complications in your personal life, you may be wise to wait before going on with your education. You do not want to use up limited financial aid while you're distracted or poorly motivated. And you don't want a weak transcript, since a weak transcript won't help you get a job and can make it difficult (or impossible) to further your education at a later date.

■ **Be very sure that you have exhausted all of your available resources before deciding that this is not the time for you to be in college.** If you're worried about money or working too much, talk to a good financial aid advisor. You might be eligible for a scholarship you've never heard of, or a loan, or additional work study. Find out what opportunities your college offers for child care, if that's a concern. Make sure you don't just need more rest, or eyeglasses, or to take one fewer course per term. Don't let one instructor or course stop you. If the only instructor for a required course is offensive to you, see if an evening or distance education section taught by another instructor is available at your college or at another nearby college.

REALITY CHECK

> A good student is someone who has learned how to learn from anyone.—Richard Watson

- **Remember, when you enroll in college you are asking to be evaluated and certified as competent according to other people's standards.** That is why a college degree is characterized as part of your formal education. Standards, practices, and curricula are formalized. Part of the social value of a college degree is the expectation of consistency and the conformity associated with it. This is arbitrary in much the same way that requiring you to drive on the right side of a two-way street is arbitrary. Certainly you could drive just as well, perhaps even more comfortably, on the left side of the street—if you were the only one on the street.

- **Learning is your responsibility.** The great philosophical teacher Socrates insisted that the teacher's task is to draw knowledge out of the pupil—not to pour information into "an empty vessel." If you approach your formal education as an active participant, not only are you more likely to learn more, you are also less likely to lay all blame on your teachers, textbooks, and courses when you encounter difficulty.

- **You probably lack the time and ability to change your teachers—and you don't need to.** Although you can help most of your teachers be better teachers by being a committed, helpful, and attentive student, you probably cannot change any of them. If you think about it, you'll realize that you are least likely to change the very worst teachers. But that's okay because:

  - **You can learn virtually any subject from virtually any teacher.** The fact of the matter—which students and professors hate to acknowledge—is that good teaching is not necessary for college success. How do we know this? We know because most of us have survived bad teaching already. We know this because we also know of students who fail in the presence of excellent teaching. We know this because, in most of our classes, some students thrive regardless of the teacher. And at this point it doesn't even matter what constitutes good and bad teaching. Different reactions to the same teacher are bedrock facts of formal education.

■ **Don't confuse bad teaching with bad teachers.** If your teacher degrades you or others, engages in sexual harassment, or expresses bigotry or prejudice to a degree that inhibits learning, you will need to take appropriate action. You should consult with a trusted counselor or other knowledgeable individual in such a serious case. Your remedies will range from talking things over with the teacher to going to the department head or a higher-level administrator in very serious situations. If the problem is a serious personality or teaching-style clash, you may have to choose between evils: sticking it out and doing your best, or dropping the class and taking it later from a different instructor. When you just cannot get along with a teacher, take appropriate, informed action on your own behalf.

■ **Not all courses are entertaining, and not all entertaining professors are good teachers.** It is unreasonable to expect your professors to entertain you. That is not their job. Besides, persuasive power, charm, and charisma are unrelated to the quality of the lesson or message they sell. Since you are in college to learn how to think well for yourself, you will need to evaluate what you're taught; it's tempting to be less critical of likable characters. More fundamentally, life itself is not always "entertaining," although I do believe that it is almost always interesting to interested minds. In some languages, "to bore" is a reflexive verb. You would say, for instance, "I bore myself in chemistry class," rather than, "Chemistry is boring." Boredom is in the mind of the impatient, incurious, or self-absorbed beholder. In any event, being bored is not a good excuse for not studying.

■ **A college degree is a minimal qualification for many opportunities; it is not, however, a necessary or sufficient condition for financial or social success, nor for personal happiness.** We know this because the world is chock-full of unhappy college graduates and happy college graduates. And we know this on a much deeper level because we have all been disappointed after acquiring some longed-for goal—just as we have all been surprised by our own positive reactions to some dreaded event, interpersonal encounter, or tough circumstance.

THE NEED FOR CERTIFICATION

While it is certainly true that what constitutes "a college education" is always somewhat arbitrary, always a "work in progress," always "under revision," it is also true that one of the social expectations of formal academic certifications is a core of conformity. A city planning commission has a right to expect that any new engineering graduates it hires possess a core of experiences, skills, and capacities common to "being an engineer." You have a right to expect that your environmental ethics professor has a degree in philosophy with an emphasis on environmental studies, not, say, a degree in sociology, chemistry, or arithmetic.

Without a common core of standards, a degree in engineering from an accredited college wouldn't tell us any more about your qualifications for designing a bridge than a letter from your third grade pal testifying to the neat bridges you constructed as a child. Now we all know about mediocre and incompetent doctors, lawyers, engineers, certified diesel mechanics, accountants, retinal surgeons, bookkeepers, pharmacists, teachers, computer technicians, amanuenses, nurse anesthetists, and (gasp) philosophy professors. And we've all wondered: "How on earth did she ever pass the bar?" "Who hired him?" "I thought you had to be pretty sharp to graduate from Bigshot University. Was I ever wrong."

So what does this prove? Only that colleges and universities, bar exams, board certifiers—like life itself—are not perfect. What it does not prove, much less justify, is the cynical and naïve notion that all standards are trivial and arbitrary, much less that we are qualified to certify ourselves.

HOW TO SET AND ACHIEVE
REALISTIC GOALS

- **Identify your strengths and weaknesses as objectively as possible.** You can do this informally or go to the college counseling center for career interest and skills testing.

- **Take advantage of your school's career center.** There are probably many career options that you are not aware of. Get some expert help in identifying them.

- **Respect your interests.** If you've always hated school, don't choose a major that requires years of it. If you've never liked children, don't plan to become a primary or secondary schoolteacher just because teaching jobs happen to be plentiful.

■ **Respect your talents.** Take advantage of your natural abilities. If you're a natural socializer and conversationalist who's always been able to make people feel comfortable, and who can relate to practically anybody, you may be happier as a teacher or social worker than working alone as a research chemist or forest ranger. Be creative as you explore your options. A natural socializer might become a happy, first-rate hotel manager or cruise ship entertainment director instead of a teacher or social worker. On the other hand, maybe you've always been good with details, even as a child. You like order and instinctively arrange things logically. Academic and career areas that are subject to creative disarray and require subjective interpretation may not be your best choice. Drama, literature, or working with small children may frustrate you, but accounting, office management, or computer processing may not.

■ **When you have no clear direction, experiment.** Take any classes that interest you for two or three terms. See if they show a pattern. If they do, fashion your newly identified interests into a workable major. If absolutely nothing interests you, consider taking a break from college.

■ **Base your immediate goals on your current life circumstances.** Realistically consider family obligations, job requirements, the demands of specific courses, transportation needs (and time), and so forth, as you plan your educational strategy.

■ **Superman and Superwoman are fictional characters. They don't exist in real life.** You may discover that your state of mind and performance significantly improve by taking one less class a term, or working five fewer hours a week. While a certain amount of tension can be good for you, too much can result in overload and inefficiency.

■ **Remember that you can always change your mind.**

TIME MANAGEMENT

By the end of the second week of the term you should have a general idea of how much time you'll need for each of your classes. Educators disagree about how much out-of-class time you should budget for every hour of scheduled class time. For many years, experts recommended 2 to 3 hours of study for every hour spent in class.

That's a minimum of 24 to 36 hours per week for 12 semester-units (or 30 to 45 hours per week for 15 units). Yet the 2004 National Survey of Student Engagement found that most students don't come anywhere near that average, even at residential colleges. Only 11% of full-time students reported studying 25 or more hours per week; 44% said that they spend 10 or fewer hours studying, reading, writing, and otherwise preparing for classes. More striking yet, an earlier survey found that 19% of the full-time freshmen and 20% of the full-time seniors surveyed said that they only devote 1 to 5 hours a week to preparing for classes. What a sad commentary on some students' willingness to settle for the bare minimum.

So how much should you study? There's no precise formula, obviously. Some academic programs involve a lot of in-class studying and practice and others require a great deal of out-of-class work. And, of course, individual needs and capacities vary.

Then there's the matter of what you expect out of college (which means out of yourself while you're in college). If your goals are crudely pragmatic, getting "good enough" grades will be "good enough" and anything extra is just that—extra. But suppose that you want good grades and a good education, not just a good-looking transcript? What if you want to be more than a "good enough" person living a "good enough" life? If that's the case, you'll want to learn as much as you can while you're in college. When that's the case, out-of-class preparation will be less of a chore and more of an opportunity—because studying and learning and growing are your main college goals, not just getting by with "good enough."

> Academic counselors report that failure to establish and stick to a regular study schedule is the most common characteristic shared by students with poor grades or who drop out of college.

Filling in the simple form on the next page will give you an idea of how important it is to take time to make time if you want to get the most out of college—and yourself.

ESTABLISH A TIME BUDGET

(YOU HAVE 168 HOURS TO SPEND EACH WEEK)

Total hours spent on campus per week
(time in class, at team practices and games,
student government, in the library, labs)   _____

_____ hours × _____ units for out-of-class study   _____

Total hours worked per week   _____

_____ hours for sleep × 7 nights   _____

Total hours per week for necessities
(cooking, eating, shopping, bathing,
laundry, yard work, etc.)   _____

Total hours per week for family duties
(driving children to various activities, helping
with homework, helping other relatives,
attending church, and so forth)   _____

Total hours per week for exercise   _____

Total commuting hours per week   _____

TOTAL OBLIGATED HOURS PER WEEK   _____

TOTAL HOURS IN A WEEK   168
                                                        _____

MINUS TOTAL OBLIGATED HOURS   − _____

EQUALS FREE TIME PER WEEK   _____

2

Changing What You Can

The wise Hasidic Rabbi Zusya once said, "When I get to heaven, they will not ask me, Why were you not Moses?, they will ask me, Why were you not Zusya?"

It can be frustrating when other people get better grades than you do without studying as much as you do. But the harsh fact is that the only value someone else's grades and study habits have for you is informational. If you can learn something from them, that will improve your comprehension skills and performance. If not, your best bet is to ignore the seeming injustice of it all.

This kind of accommodation is not the same thing as selling-out. It is grounded in academic realty. As a rule, students don't get to write or individualize their tests and assignments. Act the role of the wise student. Don't get trapped in the role of resentful would-be instructor or surly, unappreciated know-it-all. Respectfully exert what influence you can to improve your courses, but learn when to cease in these efforts and get on with doing as well as you can, given the particular demands of the course.

- **Don't punish yourself.** If a course is truly beyond your current abilities, or the instructor is demeaning, unprofessional, unprepared, and so forth, get out.

- **Don't shortchange yourself.** If you've been attending class and keeping up with assignments, trust your gut reactions. Go ahead, ask the questions that occur to you during lecture, make thoughtful comments. Give yourself credit for being able to identify issues that need clarification. Even if your instructor modifies or corrects what you say, you will have learned something, reinforced your self-respect, and polished your skills at rational discourse. How can you lose with that combination?

- **In any area where you are experiencing frustration and difficulty, consider a fresh approach.** If you've been studying philosophy after dinner, try studying at some other time. Try sitting in a different seat. Change the way you take notes. The point is, if things aren't working well, don't be too quick to dismiss alternatives. A change that seems silly or unpromising can surprise you. (Of course, if the new approach makes things worse, stop using it.) I know this sounds obvious and too simple, but you'd be surprised at how many students refuse to try new approaches because they prejudge them as unhelpful. Working hard sends yourself a signal that you are serious about your education and are willing to work hard for it.

- **Not all compromises involve your very essence.** Distinguish between accommodating yourself to the unavoidable inequities of academic life and serious unethical inequalities.

As long as you have to defend the imaginary self that you think is important, you will lose your peace of heart. As soon as you compare that shadow with the shadows of other people, you lose all joy, because you have begun to trade in unrealities, and there is no joy in things that do not exist.—Thomas Merton

---

FALSE COMPARISONS

Shortly after the invention of the steam engine, the railroad companies began to replace steel drivers with steam-powered machines that would ultimately put thousands of men out of work. According to a famous folk song, a man named John Henry challenged one of the new machines to a spike-driving contest, and "won." Swinging a hammer in each hand, the powerful John Henry drove more spikes than the machine. According to the song, John Henry was so exhausted from the effort that he "laid down his hammer and he died."

Many people see this story in terms of one man's courage in the fight against the replacement of human beings by machines. There's another lesson, too. We can kill ourselves trying to be what we're not. John Henry was not a machine. He could not be expected to do a machine's work. No amount of desire, courage, or righteousness could change the harsh reality of John Henry's relation to the new machine.

You may have untapped potential and room to grow, but you are a particular individual and no other. You cannot become the student sitting next to you, your mother, pal, teacher, or fictionalized ideal. Learn from others, but don't condemn yourself for not being them. Don't exhaust yourself trying to be someone you're not.

If you're interested in this issue of "becoming yourself," you can read more about it in Chapter 7, "The Naturalist: Aristotle," in my philosophy textbook, *Archetypes of Wisdom,* Sixth Edition.

> Many [people] . . . never become the [person] who is called for by all the circumstances of their individual lives. They waste their years in vain efforts to be some other [person]. . . . For many absurd reasons, they are convinced that they are obliged to become somebody else. . . . They wear out their minds and bodies in a hopeless endeavor to have somebody else's experiences or write somebody else's poems or express somebody else's spirituality.—Thomas Merton

■ **Sometimes it takes courage to keep on doing something, and sometimes it takes courage to quit (especially if others will be disappointed).** It's sometimes better to quit early than it is to quit later. Of course, this principle has a corollary that works in the other direction. You shouldn't expect others to "carry you," or meet responsibilities that you are capable of meeting. So be sure that you're quitting for good reasons and not just to avoid hard work.

■ **Resist comparisons that lead to resentment.** We all know that life is not particularly fair. Resentment won't improve your grades—but it can pollute your emotions in a way that seriously interferes with good study habits.

■ **March to your own beat.** If other people pressure you to proceed at a pace that's inappropriate for you, if they make fun of you for lacking certain skills, remind yourself that they will not suffer if you have to drop out of college, and that they won't pay your student loans if you can't keep up. In other words, **you** are the one who will pay the price if you fail to meet **their** expectations. Your friends and family shouldn't expect you to make their credit card payments—and they shouldn't expect you to make their "life payments." If they do expect you to, resist in the best, most honorable way that you can.

"REACH WHAT YOU CANNOT"

In his remarkable memoir *Report to Greco,* Nikos Kazantzakis describes a dream in which, as a little boy, he encounters his grandfather. Looking down at the child, the grandfather asks, "Do you remember what I taught you, Nikos?" "Yes, Grandfather," the boy answers. "Reach what you can." "No!" the old man replies. "Reach what you cannot!" The point, of course, is that one way to enrich ourselves is to push ourselves toward the kinds of excellence that come from hard work dedicated to worthy goals.

■ **Nurture a commitment to excellence; determine always to seek your own highest level, given an honest assessment of your actual circumstances.** Remind yourself that you are not going to college to impress others or to impress yourself. You are going to college to nourish your finer attributes, one of which is a willingness to demand high standards for yourself. Think about a time when you "surpassed yourself" and refused to succumb to tempting distractions or to the "easier, softer way." Think about a time when you persisted even though part of you cried out to quit or settle for the minimal standard. Perhaps you stuck it out through the grueling weeks of August football drills, stuck it out when you felt like collapsing. Perhaps you signed up for tutoring help in a difficult algebra course, rather than dropping out. Perhaps you retyped an English essay when you realized that you could do better. And perhaps after all that effort, you didn't make the team, or got a D in Algebra or English. You got something else, too, something more important in the long run: a reinforced commitment to yourself, a reinforced commitment to high aspirations and quality effort. You "reached what you cannot reach." Far better to fail now and then at worthy goals, goals that enhance your spirit, than to succeed at the trite and safe. (Dangerous advice, perhaps, but then philosophy has always been dangerous.)

■ **Nurture a commitment to excellence by going to the best college you can—given an honest assessment of yourself.** We have to be careful here not to be seduced by twin delusions. The first delusion is the notion that only name-brand colleges are good enough. The advantages of such colleges are well known: competitive standards, world-class facilities and faculties, valuable social contacts, and a stimulating environment. But none of these assets matters much if a particular college is not a "good fit" for you. World-class scholars are not necessarily world-class teachers. Then, too, at many colleges most undergraduate courses are taught by teaching assistants and junior faculty. They may be superb teachers, but the point here is about getting a realistic idea of what a given college has to offer you on a real-life, day-to-day basis. The second delusion is the idea that convenience matters most when selecting a college. I have seen many students sell themselves short by choosing local colleges just because they are nearby, easy to get into, and relatively inexpensive. "Wait, a minute!" you're probably thinking, "What's so bad about a convenient, cheap college that I can get into?" Perhaps there is nothing wrong with it, but if you choose a college just to avoid inconvenience you may be reinforcing a tendency to put comfort over quality.

- **There is no magic fix for getting a first-rate education.** Whatever route you take, plan to study hard, keep your promises, and do your part—you'll be an inspiration to others and rightfully proud of yourself.

- **Think of going to college as your primary job.** Job requirements include regular attendance; doing assignments; spending money on supplies instead of pizza and DVDs; listening to ideas you don't like or have no personal interest in; taking good notes; paying attention; and studying, studying, studying.

- **Remind yourself that the full price of your education includes more than the monetary cost of fees and supplies.** You must pay with time, effort, and a temporarily modified social life. You will get the best education by paying full price. Trying to "have it all" commonly results in frustration, anxiety, fatigue, and increased risk of failure.

The typical three-unit semester course meets for less than 48 hours. That's right: less than two full days of class time. That's an average of a paltry 70 to 80 days for a bachelor's degree. If you study three hours for every class time hour, you'll add only six days, bringing the total to a week and one day. Generously allowing another two full weeks for total time spent on term papers and so forth, one three-unit class involves a total of three weeks and one day. And for those students who do not study three hours for every hour spent in class, a three-unit course takes even less time. The total number of hours stays the same even for students who take five or six years to get a so-called four-year degree. The extra time is usually the result of taking fewer units per term. Even adding in the hours needed for out-of-class preparation, and the dollar cost of tuition, supplies, room and board, a college education is quite a bargain—particularly at public colleges.

- **Regularly tell yourself that being a college student is only a temporary condition.** College may seem to go on forever, but it doesn't. You will have a "real life" someday. (And if you're like many of us, you'll look back on your years in college as "the good old days.")

A COLLEGE EDUCATION *IS* WORTH THE EFFORT

Lack of a college degree is a burden in today's economy, no matter what else affects your chances for a satisfying job. Most students understandably go to college in the hopes that having a college degree will lead to a high-paying, satisfying job. Unfortunately, things aren't that simple. As more and more people graduate from college, the marketplace significance of having a college education diminishes. Ironically, this means that the significance of **not** having a college education **increases.** As a college degree becomes the minimum, the lack of a college degree becomes a serious impediment to future job seekers. And, clearly, as more people earn college degrees, the quality of your transcript matters more and more.

- **Think of your transcript as a kind of "credit report."** It takes 10 years to overcome the negative effects of a bankruptcy on a person's credit history. It can also take many years to overcome a weak college transcript. What makes a transcript "weak"? For one thing, a low grade point average is a detriment on a transcript. So are lots of withdrawals and lots of fluff courses. When employers and graduate school admissions officers look at a big pile of transcripts and applications, they need criteria for awarding their limited jobs or scholarships. They actively look for reasons to exclude applicants. Consequently, just about everything in your application packet is important: letters of recommendation, work history, hobbies—and the courses you took and the grades you received.

- **All the effort and careful attention will pay off.** To begin with the philosophical point first, regardless of the kind of job you get, your college education should provide you with reasoning skills, interests, cultural baggage, and character traits that will help you cope with life. On the socioeconomic front, Lunenfeld and Lunenfeld report in *College Basics,* that Anthony Patrick Carnevale, Ph.D., of the American Society for Training and Development, compared the potential lifetime earnings of two students, one without and one with

17

a college degree. Dr. Carnevale calculated that the college degree would be worth about $631,000 in additional income. Some economists believe Dr. Carnevale's estimate is low and that the dollar-value of a college education is closer to $1,000,000.

■ **What about all those Ph.D.'s driving cabs and flipping burgers?** Keep in mind that jobs requiring a doctorate are still relatively rare. Many people pursue a Ph.D., hoping to get one of the few jobs in their narrow specialty. Associate of Arts, vocational degrees, and Bachelor of Arts degrees are in far greater demand. A college degree provides a greater range of job opportunities, not a guaranteed job. Expecting a guarantee is unrealistic. Landing a good job depends on luck and such individual characteristics as your willingness to be flexible at the start of your career, your choice of major, and your willingness to live where the good jobs in your field are located. More importantly, some very satisfied people (with and without Ph.D.'s) drive cabs and flip burgers. **Socrates (c. 470–399 BCE)** was a brick mason, **Lao-tzu (c. 575 BCE)** was a low-level bureaucrat, and **Baruch Spinoza (1632–1677)** was a lens grinder—three examples of wise people who deliberately chose very ordinary jobs.

Good habits are good habits—in college and in "real life." Going to college can help you develop and refine your life-management skills. To survive and thrive during a typical college education you must learn to concentrate on what others are saying. You will learn to learn from people whether or not you like them or find them attractive or interesting. You will learn to "perform" in the face of criticism. You will be encouraged to get to "work" on time, and you will learn how to deal with different kinds of "bosses" (teachers) and "coworkers" (other students). You will learn computer skills, researching skills, and critical thinking skills. And if you do not resist, you will learn to enjoy learning and to value hard work in the pursuit of excellence.

All in all, quite a bargain.

A NOTE OF ENCOURAGEMENT
FOR PART-TIME STUDENTS

According to the American Council on Education, there are more part-time students than ever before. Today, more than 40% of all college students are part-timers, and analysts expect the proportion of part-time students to increase in the foreseeable future. At many colleges, part-time students outnumber full-time students many times over. If you are one of these students, do your very best to make college a priority. Here are some ways to do that:

- **Regularly focus your attention on the importance and value of your long-term goals.** Consult your list of reasons for going to college. Add to it. Remind yourself why you are juggling family life, a job, social activities, and college: You want a satisfying life for yourself and any family you may have, and you have realistically determined that a college education is necessary for that life.

- **Read and listen to inspiring stories about others who have struggled to get ahead.** Think of relatives who have worked hard to support you. Think of people you admire who worked hard and struggled for a mighty goal.

- **Put your frustrations in perspective.** You may be very, very, very busy, and very, very, very poor, and very, very, very stressed-out at times, but people have suffered and are suffering as much or more than you, and surviving, and even growing. This suggestion is not meant to trivialize your hardships, but to help you endure and master them. If life has dealt you a more difficult hand than others, you have all the more reason to persist with your studies and give yourself every opportunity to have a better future than you will probably have if you drop out of college.

- **Take advantage of every support system you can find.** Many colleges provide day care for students' children. See if you qualify. Most colleges have tutorial centers, reading, writing, science, math labs, computer centers, and health clinics. Many also offer special, overlooked scholarships for returning students, unmarried mothers, people who are going to college after military service or retirement or to learn a new trade, scholarships for first-generation college students, members of different ethnic and religious groups, and so on. Ask around and shop around until you find a good advisor or counselor. Don't overlook grants and formal gifts that provide cash for textbooks, supplies, transportation, and living expenses.

- **A six- or seven-year degree is still a degree—and a good education is what you're ultimately after.** If it takes you longer to graduate than it takes full-time students, so be it. No matter how angry or frustrated this may make you, don't let it stop you. The Stoic writer **Seneca (c. 4 BCE–65 CE)** said, "The greater the torment, the greater shall the glory be." If you persist, you will not only have a college degree or certificate, but you will have become a stronger, wiser, more appreciative human being in the process. That's quite a payoff.

All things excellent are as difficult as they are rare.—Baruch Spinoza

---

STUDENT WISDOM REVIEW

▪ **Activate to motivate.** The philosophical amanuensis, M. L. Malone, uses this formula as a reminder that—paradoxically and frustratingly—we must often "act as if" before we "feel like it." That is, spontaneously inspired motivation does not always arrive in time. Consequently, we are better served to take helpful, responsible, reasonable action when we need to, rather than wait until we want to. Fortunately, action is itself a tonic, and almost always reduces, if it does not completely abolish, lack of energy, lack of commitment, lack of motivation.

▪ **HALT!** That's not an order, it's an acronym, an easily remembered abbreviation for the formula: "Don't let yourself get too **H**ungry, too **A**ngry, too **L**onely, or too **T**ired." The Classical Greeks and Romans believed in "a sound mind in a sound body" and contemporary science suggests that they were right. We learn best when our basic physical, emotional, and mental needs are all met.

▪ **Take the "walking cure."** Even relatively mild exercise reduces anxiety and increases our sense of well-being and happiness. Some psychologists even treat mild depression with exercise and attribute some anxieties to "an overactive mind in an underactive body."

▪ **When in doubt, talk it out.** Sometimes the simple act of discussing problems generates solutions. Even if it doesn't, it almost always provides mental and emotional relief, and restores balance and perspective.

▪ **Meet your obligations to yourself as well as to your family, friends, and employer in a balanced way.** You are entitled to a good education and you do not need to feel guilty for taking time for yourself to get one. You also have other responsibilities. If you fail to meet them adequately, you may find yourself distracted by guilt. If you fail to give yourself enough time to learn, you may find yourself drained by anger and resentment. Balance can be difficult to find, but it pays off.

- **Be flexible in all but the essentials.** Stick to your guns on important matters, but cut yourself some slack on all others.

- **Study when you can and study regularly, not just before major tests.** Not only will this improve your grades, skills, and comprehension, it will reinforce the message that learning is an integral part of your life, not something you do only under pressure. It also reduces unhealthy anxiety—a real killer.

- **Do not wait to study until weekends or immediately before tests or just before assignments are due.** Even if your grades don't suffer when you fall into the clutches of procrastination and last-minute-itis, you will have robbed yourself of processing information for long-term retention and mastery. You will add anxiety to your already busy life. You will deprive yourself of full participation in class, since you won't be familiar with the material as it is covered.

- **Make a supreme effort to read every assignment at least once before class.** You may not be able to study every page of all of your assignments before every class, but you should at least review your texts before every class meeting. Naturally, the more time you can devote to preclass reading, the better, but even a quick reading of assigned material will pay off. You will be familiar with the purpose of each lecture or discussion. You will be more comfortable asking questions if you are familiar with the material (and hence more willing to ask questions). You will feel less anxious when you are prepared, and you will remember and understand better than if you were tense or uninformed.

- **Get everything you are paying for.** Have you ever been glad to discover that a class has been canceled or let out early? Sure, a change of pace is great once in a while. It can be invigorating. You cannot help it when classes are canceled, but you can resist the defeatist attitude of thinking "Ugh! I have to go to class" when they are not. To that end, don't drag yourself to class as if you were heading to your doom. Attend eagerly, grateful for the opportunity to learn something new in a pleasant environment. College is the only "commodity" I know of where people are happy when they don't get everything they're paying for.

- **Take classes from the best—not the easiest—instructors you can.** It's a waste of your time to take classes just because they're easy. That's a way of stealing your own time. Avoiding challenges diminishes your abilities and impedes self-respect. The best way to find good instructors is to ask around. Ask everybody you meet to recommend instructors. You'll quickly recognize the names of the best.

■ **Take at least one class you're afraid of—and stick it out.** Simply completing a challenging class will boost your sense of self-respect. It will show you that you have drive and discipline. And you might discover new interests and abilities. Remember, you can do difficult things!

■ **Take at least one class for the sheer joy of it.** Break free of the trap of the drudge: the student whose whole education is serious and calculating, allowing no room for failure (defined as anything less than an A). A shriveled life is a pretty high price to pay for a 4.0 GPA (grade point average). If you view college as something to "get over with," you will rob yourself of the personal enrichment that should be part of any real education. There is nothing wrong with the practical, job-preparation part of contemporary higher education. But so much more is possible, if you want it.

■ **Drop classes only when absolutely necessary.** A high GPA accompanied by a high percentage of dropped courses is a red flag to employers as well as to admission committees of professional schools. Do well the first time.

■ **Feel free to pick your own major: Remember, it's your life.** The late mythologist Joseph Campbell used to say, "There's no greater tragedy than to get to the top of the ladder and realize you're on the wrong wall."

■ **When you feel like you'll never get done, think of this Buddhist proverb: "The journey is the destination."** There is no rule against enjoying philosophy and college. Besides, you certainly do not want to be the kind of person who would say, "Well, that's it for me. I've learned enough. My education is complete."

GOING TO COLLEGE IS LIKE
BUYING LETTUCE

When you get frustrated and resent paying the price, review this lesson from the *Enchiridion* of the Stoic philosopher **Epictetus (c. 50–130):**

> You will be unjust then and insatiable, if you do not part with the price, in return for which . . . things are sold, and if you wish to obtain them for nothing. Well, what is the price of lettuces? An obulus perhaps. If then a man gives up the obulus and receives the lettuces, and if you do not give up the obulus

and do not receive the lettuces, do not suppose that you receive less than he who has got the lettuces; for as he has the lettuces, so you have the obulus which you did not give . . .

If another student "gives up the obulus" by devoting time to philosophy, and by studying harder and more frequently than you do, don't compound your problems by resenting his or her better grade. He or she has a good grade in philosophy; you have your obulus (time used for other things).

Perhaps you're thinking, "But it is not so simple. I have a job and family—the other student doesn't. It's easy for her to study. I'd like to see what kind of grades she would get in my circumstances." Put that curiosity to rest and review the earlier section on false comparisons. Remind yourself that you will never be able to see what kind of grades another student would get in your circumstances because you are an essential component of what makes your circumstances your circumstances. (And, of course, you really don't know how hard or easy it is for others to study.)

Whether or not life is "fair" is a deep philosophical problem that you have a lifetime to wrestle with. Right now, you need to maximize your actual circumstances. Think carefully about the "obuluses" in your life. Are you perhaps trying to "clip the coin a trifle" and not pay the full price? If so, you need to decide if the quality of your education (and all that is connected with it) warrants more effort and sacrifice while you're in college. If you are truly out of resources, and cannot pay the price, then you need to deal with that.

It's probably not fair that some people have it easier than others. But if life is not fair, then there's no reason to waste time harping on it, or foolishly waiting for someone or something to make it fair. Maybe they shouldn't charge a whole obulus for a lettuce, but until you are in a position to open a market or grow your own lettuce, about all you can do is decide to keep the obulus or acquire the lettuce.

As long as you're paying for a college education—and every student pays something—you might as well pay what it costs to get a good one. And you might as well get your obulus's worth by studying and learning. Otherwise, you'll be like a man who pays an obulus for a head of lettuce and then only nibbles on a few leaves and then lets it rot. What a waste—of an obulus and a head of lettuce.

What students bring to college matters more than what colleges bring to students.—Robert J. Samuelson

---

THE BIGGEST *AVOIDABLE* MISTAKES
COLLEGE STUDENTS MAKE

- **Not making college a priority.** This can be difficult if you are a part-time student, or have family obligations, or work long hours at a job—but not making college a priority is one of the worst things you can do to your chances for a good education.

- **Poor course selection.** Consult experienced students, and select courses by professors, not just course names.

- **Signing up for too many or too few classes.** Freshmen should be especially careful not to overload their schedules the first term. At the same time, taking too few classes can lead to dropping out of college if progress toward a degree takes too long. Ironically, taking too few classes can be worse than having a full schedule, if your light load gives you a false sense of security that makes sticking to a study schedule difficult. Also, taking too few credit courses can result in a loss of financial aid.

- **Poor study habits.** Poor study habits include not studying enough, studying when distracted or tired, studying in bed, studying under the influence of drugs.

- **Making false economies.** Given the money-focused nature of this culture, it's not surprising that college students try to save as much money as possible. But sometimes saving money gets to be pretty expensive. One of the worst trade-offs you can make is trying to get by without purchasing your own copies of all course materials: textbooks, workbooks, recommended readings. Studying is hard enough, without the added complication of trying to budget additional travel time to get to the library to use reserve copies of the text—only to find that they're unavailable. Book-sharing partners change their minds or schedules. False economies are particularly destructive when they're the result of indulgences such as spending limited resources for fancy wheels for your truck or expensive hairdos, and the like, instead of investing those resources in a good education when it is offered. No one is suggesting that you live like a monk (but in some cases, a simpler, more disciplined lifestyle might be a wise idea for a while).

- **Social extremism.** You may be tempted to drop out of college if you delete all social involvement and fun from your life. You may be tempted to drop out of college if you are too busy socializing and having "the college experience." Don't lose sight of the fact that getting a good education is the most important part of that experience, and being well educated includes learning how to find a balance between workaholism and dissolute self-indulgence.

▪ **Sophomore ego.** The "sophomore ego" is an inflated sense of superiority that some college students retain long after they stop being sophomores. This mind-set occurs when the natural joy and delight of being new to higher education, of having optimistic, idealistic goals, and of sometimes seeing through hypocrisy and pernicious compromise are misinterpreted as signs of profound insight and wisdom. The sophomore ego is ready to fix the world. Often, the sophomore ego's concerns are real and important: the environment, social justice, poverty. But dogmatism (unquestioning faith in the correctness and superiority of our own ideas) is not just a hindrance to learning, it often alienates others, making it more difficult to communicate our ideas to them.

> However much you study, you cannot know without action.—Saadi of Shiraz

3

Self-Respect and Academic Ethics

You will demand much of your teachers,
but what you get is your responsibility.
WILLIAM H. ARMSTRONG

I distinguish between self-respect and self-esteem in a way that is not particularly popular. It rests on subtle and complex notions regarding objectivity, self, character, and on the notion that we each have a basic moral obligation to respect everyone we come into contact with, including ourselves. I can only present a sketch of it here, but I believe that even if you reject my distinction or are troubled by some of my suggestions, I believe that reflecting on the possibility that we have duties of self-respect will still prove worthwhile.

To begin on a practical level, an essential component of any good learning environment is mutual respect. Teachers and students are equally entitled to decent treatment from one another. As a student, you have special responsibilities and obligations to yourself, your classmates, and your teachers. (Teachers also have special ethical obligations, but this is a student manual.)

Self-respect, as I am using the term, differs from self-esteem. Self-esteem refers to our opinions of ourselves. It is entirely subjective.

The harmful psychological effects of excessively low self-esteem are well known and highly publicized. You've probably discussed "self-esteem issues" in other courses, perhaps even in grade school or high school. For all of its importance to our well-being, however, self-esteem is not connected to reality checking.

Too often, too little attention has been paid to the equally harm-ful effects that result from a lack of self-respect. In contrast to self-esteem, self-respect is the quality of valuing ourselves for the right reasons. Self-respect begins with a commitment to truth, to objectiv-ity, and to integrity. Self-respect cannot be reduced to subjective states because just as it is possible for a highly competent, talented individual to possess unreasonably low self-esteem, so, too, is it possible for lazy, corrupt, or cruel individuals to have unreasonably high self-esteem. Our subjective responses do not always reflect objective conditions.

Focusing on reasonable self-respect helps us avoid the trap of paying more attention to how we feel than to how we act. Self-respect is a function of personal integrity, and as such cannot be divorced from reality testing or reduced to our feelings about our-selves. This is not to say that feelings don't play a role in self-respect, only that self-respect entails (1) accurate recognition of our capacities, commitments, rights, and duties, and (2) behavior that is generally and purposefully consistent with them.

As important as our feelings about ourselves are, they do not com-pletely reflect who we really are. We may feel badly about ourselves even though we work hard, meet our responsibilities, and take good care of ourselves—and we may feel just great about ourselves while behaving irresponsibly, or even cruelly, toward ourselves and toward others.

In one of the most influential works of modern moral philoso-phy, **Immanuel Kant (1724–1804)** argued that respect for persons is one of the three basic principles that serve as the foundation of our specific moral obligations. In a famous passage, Kant frames what is known as the Principle of Dignity as an imperative: *"Act so that you treat humanity, whether in your own person or in that of another, always as* *an end and never as a means only."* (If you'd like to read more about Kant, see Chapter 12 of my introductory textbook *Archetypes of Wisdom,* Sixth Edition, or any number of other excellent introductory philosophy or ethics texts.)

I am particularly impressed—and convinced—by Kant's insistence that we have a general, basic obligation not to treat ourselves as means only. To treat something as a means is to value it as a way to accomplish or acquire something else, that is, to value that thing extrinsically. When we treat something as an end in and of itself, we value it intrinsically—of and for itself.

If you buy an antique vase because you believe it will increase in monetary value, your ultimate goal (end) is making money. The vase is a means to that end. You could just as easily have bought a spoon or quilt, if they could have more efficiently accomplished your goal. If, on the other hand, you buy an antique vase because you admire its beauty and have no intention of selling it later, then for you, the vase is an end–in–itself, not a means to something else. That specific vase has intrinsic value for you, value unique to that vase. (Of course, the vase may have both extrinsic and intrinsic value for you.)

Another, more significant way to grasp means-ends, extrinsic-intrinsic distinctions is to consider persons. If you are fortunate enough to love someone, that person has intrinsic value for you. I love my wife because she is exactly who she is—not as a means to financial security, not as a source of emotional support, or physical comfort. She may, indeed, be a means to many ends, but my love for her is not dependent on those ends. In other words, if she gets sick or loses her job, she does not "lose her value" the way a vehicle does when it malfunctions or an investment when it goes bad.

Kant realized that we all serve as means to various ends for one another. Teachers are means to credits in philosophy courses for their students, and students are means to a job for their teachers. My plumber is a means to a repaired toilet for me, and I am a means to an enormous income for her. But Kant warned against reducing persons (ourselves as well as others) to mere means, to means only. His arguments are complex, and philosophers disagree over their soundness. Nonetheless, he makes a valuable observation, one echoed in other moral, religious, and philosophical works: Persons are not things. In Kantian language, you and I possess intrinsic worth (dignity) that entitles us to fundamental moral respect—and that obligates us to show respect for ourselves and others.

When we treat others with disrespect, we ignore or harm their dignity. We can do this in dramatic ways (murder, sexual assault, gross insults) or in more or less subtle ways (wasting other people's time, manipulating them, lying, and cheating). We can also disrespect ourselves through substance abuse, sexual promiscuity, reducing ourselves to "workaholics," "fame-aholics," or "grade-aholics."

As a college student you have a basic obligation to yourself and to the community that supports your college to get as much value from your education as possible. On the most primitive level, you simply owe it to yourself not to waste your own time. On a more social level, no public college student, no student on financial aid, no student participating in any program funded by taxes, no student supported by his or her parents or others ever pays for the complete financial cost of a college degree. This is especially true at state colleges and universities. Tuition does not cover the financial cost to the college of your education. Thus—directly or indirectly—your college education is supported by a larger community.

The win-win way to show respect and gratitude to that community is to get yourself educated by doing everything in your power to benefit from your subsidized college time. In an ideal world, this would make you happier, healthier, and employable, which, in turn, would make your family, friends, and community happier and healthier. In the real world things are murkier. Nonetheless, you are almost certain to be much better off if you make the most out of college and if you think in terms of owing yourself a great deal of solid self-respect.

Thinking in terms of self-respect instead of (or at least in addition to) self-esteem will raise your sights and encourage you to do your honest best. Most of us know of individuals who are, so it appears, proud of "getting away" with things: buying term papers, cheating on tests, having friends sign attendance sheets, never cracking (or even owning) a textbook. As we've seen, it is possible for such persons to have high self-esteem even though their attitudes and actions sow disrespect and unease all around. Cheaters annoy honest students and high rates of cheating have led some professors to ignore cheating altogether or, at the opposite extreme, to initiate totalitarian overreactions to cheating that result in hostile, chilly classroom dynamics for everyone.

No matter what you think of yourself, you are worthy of a good education. Because you are worthy of a good education, you owe it to yourself to do whatever it takes for you to be a good student. Being a good student does not require being a so-called perfect student. Some students with a 4.0 grade point average cheat themselves out of a rich well-rounded education and sane social life. You must ultimately seek your own honest counsel here. In today's competitive world, you should strive to get the highest grades you can get. But you should do so with an honest, realistic appraisal of your current life circumstances. What is realistic for a single student living with mom and dad and what is realistic for a single-parent student with two children and a full-time job are clearly not the same.

CAMPUS ETHICS

The last thing you want to do is "mediocritize" your own life. So, if for no other reason, it is in your own self-interest to nurture a wholesome campus environment. To that end, you'll want to develop habits and attitudes that enrich your educational experiences. And since the quality of your education is affected by your teachers and fellow students, you'll want to treat them with courtesy and respect.

In the end, unethical practices not only interfere with your education by fostering indolence, dishonesty, resentment, and alienation, they always cost more than they pay out. The student who somehow manages to "get away" with cheating, skimming through Cliffs Notes®, buying term papers, last-minute cramming, and poor attendance will have accomplished the tragic feat of graduating from college without an education.

See if the following guidelines don't convince you that ethical behavior has both moral and practical benefits. In other words, it is to your personal advantage to behave ethically.

- **Be courteous in class.** Discourtesy pollutes the classroom, laboratory, or athletic field. Rude comments, hostile or disinterested body language, communicating with other students during lectures or while others have the floor send messages (intentionally or not) of indifference and contempt for others and for the educational activity in progress. Discourtesy distracts and disturbs serious students, students fulfilling their obligations to themselves and the learning community. Discourtesy may also draw the kind of attention to you that negatively affects your grades.

- **Turn off your cell phone.** See the preceding guideline.

- **Don't cheat in any form.** All academic cheating is a form of theft. If cheating is widespread, it leads to general contempt for education, expertise, and certification. If many people get good grades they have not earned, the value of everyone's grade point average (and degree) is diminished. The more mediocre, marginally qualified, semiliterate college graduates there are, the less significance your degree will have because no one will know which category of graduates you fall into: informed, competent graduates, or mediocre, fraudulent graduates.

- **Keep your commitments.** Your instructor has to budget his or her time, too. When you turn in papers late or ask to take tests late, you place extra demands on that time. Be sure you have very good reasons before doing that—and if you must have special consideration, be sure to fulfill whatever optional deadline or choice your instructor allows.

- **Arrive on time and remain for the entire period—unless you've made other arrangements with your instructor.** Wandering in and out of class on your own schedule cheapens the atmosphere of the class. Leaving in the middle of class is like walking away without explanation in the middle of a conversation—not a respectful or friendly thing to do. Making the effort to arrive on time is another way of reinforcing the message to yourself that your classes and degree are important to you, and that you deserve a first-rate education and have the will to do what's necessary to get one.

- **Don't show off.** Most of us are familiar with the student-as-star. This is the individual who has plenty to say at every class meeting. When one or two students dominate class time, the rest of the class may grow resentful and tune out whenever the student-as-star has the floor. No matter how eager you are, you won't lose anything by giving less-confident students a chance to partake in class discussions, and you will contribute to the class by your courtesy. It's best to avoid the extremes of excessive shyness and excessive demands for attention.

Don't stifle genuine interest, however. If you're truly bursting with comments and questions, make arrangements to meet with your instructor during office hours or at other mutually convenient times.

- **Do give each subject a real chance—because you are always developing and never know what new, unexpected interest or path may reveal itself.** Lack of effort due to an initial lack of interest in a particular subject is guaranteed to blind you to the merits of new subjects and inhibit the discovery of as yet untapped abilities and interests that, once noted and nurtured, can add vigor and quality— even purpose—to your college years, as well as to your later life. Don't get lulled into thinking that just because you used to dislike a subject you'll always dislike it. You are changing all the time and in ways you may not always recognize right away.

- **Don't ask lazy (embarrassing) questions.** Never use class time to ask any question you can find the answer to by yourself. Don't ask questions if you have not been studying; you won't have any idea whether or not the answers are in the reading. What are lazy questions? Asking how many tests there will be when that information is stated clearly on the course syllabus that you were given the first week of class. Asking the meaning of a term that's defined in the textbook. Asking what page X is on when that information is included in the index of your textbook. When you ask lazy questions, you steal time from others.

- **Don't ask "diminishing" questions.** A "diminishing" question is any question asked to avoid doing your best. Here are some examples of commonly asked diminishing questions: Do spelling and grammar count? Do I have to buy the textbook? I don't like to type; can I just write my papers in longhand? The problem with diminishing questions is that they reinforce a concept of their asker as a lazy student trying to do as little as possible.

If this seems like an unreasonably harsh position, consider some implications of the grammar and spelling question just used as an example. Granted, many of us are poor spellers, and it would seem that subject matter (content) should count most. But do you honestly want to get away with meeting lower standards than were met by earlier generations of students (including, perhaps, your own instructor)? And if you do, what does that say about you? Why should you or your class be treated as an exceptional group that's not required to meet the highest standards? Why would you want to be exempted from the strenuous, but rewarding, effort necessary to be your very best?

Asking for special consideration due to genuine need is not the same thing as asking diminishing questions. Of course what counts as a "genuine need" is not always clear. Here, we must rely on the integrity and insight of all of the parties involved. But that's true of most practical questions.

> Here's a rule of thumb to use for identifying diminishing questions: If the chief purpose of a question is to evade hard work, high standards of achievement, or to avoid responsibilities that the asker has the ability—but not the desire—to meet, then the question diminishes the asker.

■ **Don't sign up for classes unless you are reasonably sure you will complete them.** Many colleges suffer from overcrowding. If you drop a class after the deadline to enroll in courses has passed, you've prevented anyone else from taking that course. Dropping a class is not merely a personal matter.

■ **Treat student evaluations of your professors with care.** Although you may not be aware of it, most instructors react to student evaluations. If a number of students praise a feature of the class, professors are likely to continue it. If a number of students complain about the same thing, most professors take it seriously. Student evaluations are your chance to help your professors and their future students. If you have complaints, present them in a mature manner. Personal attacks, ungrammatical diatribes, and X-rated language tend to be dismissed as the immature reactions of failing students. Be specific. Tell your professors what is good or bad about their courses and why.

■ **If you can't resist communicating with your friends during class, don't sit near them.** All discussions in class should relate to the class and be directed to the entire class (unless your instructor assigns you to small groups). Fidgeting, mumbling, or passing notes interferes with the concentration of others and deprives them of their very basic right to a congenial learning environment. It also prevents you from learning along with the rest of the class, which can increase or foster feelings of alienation, defensiveness, and boredom. (The same points apply to text messaging and web surfing.)

PLAGIARISM

Technically, any uncredited use of someone else's exact words—or a close paraphrase—constitutes plagiarism. Many scholars and scientists consider plagiarism to be the most serious of all academic "sins."

And that's understandable. Stealing others' ideas and words cuts at the very heart of academic ethics.

Professors take plagiarism seriously. Unless it's caught, plagiarized work results in students' getting credit for work they have not done and perhaps cannot do. On a social level, widespread plagiarism not only increases grade inflation, it also diminishes the worth of college degrees. As the number of poorly prepared graduates increases, everyone's diploma becomes suspect.

Submitting a term paper or essay that you did not write as if you did write it is probably the most egregious form of student plagiarism since not one single word or idea is a product of your own efforts. Unfortunately, the temptation to plagiarize is stronger today than it's ever been.

> According to George D. Kuh, director of the 2003 National Survey of Student Engagement, 87% of the 60,000 students surveyed said they knew of other students who had copied and pasted material from the Internet into papers without acknowledging that they had done so.

Grade inflation (yes, it's real) puts pressure on students to get the highest grades possible and Internet-based term-paper mills—sites that sell term papers—make buying papers easier than ever before. Word processors make it easy for busy students to cut and paste huge chunks of downloaded text. If these chunks are not offset in quotation marks and thoroughly cited via footnotes, endnotes, or in-text citations, the result is plagiarism.

> Widespread cheating by students who cut-and-paste assignments and term papers off the Web and submit them as their own threatens to graduate a whole new generation of students who've learned virtually nothing.—William Walker

In the last few years, prominent scholars have been embarrassed by accusations of plagiarism. One famous historian lost her role as a television commentator when it was revealed that one of her most popular books contained hundreds of uncredited paraphrases and verbatim quotes from another writer's less-well-known work. Similarly, a best-selling nonfiction writer became the subject of condemnatory newspaper editorials and TV commentators for "borrowing heavily" from other writers without giving them credit. A prominent classicist was fired—for "scholarly misconduct"—from his job as the chairman of the classics department of a state university when his university learned that he had plagiarized significant portions of a book. Cadets have been cashiered from military academies and students can be expelled from college for a single act of plagiarism. At some colleges, a proven case of plagiarism is noted on the plagiarist's permanent transcript.

> The label "plagiarist" can ruin a writer, destroy a scholarly career, blast a politician's chances for election, and cause the expulsion of a student from a college or university.—Richard C. Posner

As tempting as it may be to "borrow" heavily from others' work, there are pragmatic reasons not to. (That there are ethical reasons goes without saying.) Plagiarism in the form of excessive paraphrasing is unusually easy to spot because, more often than not, the writing style of the text keeps shifting back and forth from writer A to writer B to writer C. Often, the content of plagiarized passages is too sophisticated for introductory-level work or inconsistent with the student-writer's other work. In the most pathetic cases, I've seen the plagiarized work is actually poorer than the students' own writing.

> When I taught Gulliver's Travels to my "Introduction to Literature" class one year, three women turned in the same paper.—Vincent Moore

If you find that you are going back and forth between reading and writing, always consulting your text, you are in danger of excessive paraphrasing. Your best safeguard is to use separate note cards to jot down all key quotations and brief summaries of key ideas. Organize your cards and then write your paper in your own words, inserting carefully selected and cited quotes as needed.

When in doubt, play it safely and ethically by citing your sources, even if you have changed a few words here and there. If you don't know how frequently to cite (or how to cite), ask your instructor. If he or she is too busy or unwilling to help you, go to your school's writing lab or writing center. Most colleges have them. If yours does not, invest in a good style guide and study it. I have listed some style guides in the Beginning Philosopher's Bibliography at the end of this book. I've also included a simplified style guide (Appendix A) and other tips for effective critical writing in Chapter 7.

BE COOL ABOUT BEING COOL
IN SCHOOL

There is a deadly kind of "cool" attitude that's a killer in college. It's the sort of icy cool that reflects aloofness, disdain, and detachment. Being cool that way can really make it hard to get the most out of college. That's the kind of cool this section is about.

- **Being too concerned with being cool can make it harder to succeed in college than it might otherwise be.** Being "cool" sometimes manifests itself as adopting a style that is deliberately unresponsive, aloof, antiestablishment, and distant—detached and "in control" of every gesture, word, and emotion. That kind of cool sits in the back of the classroom. It slouches and smirks; it sleeps in class; it wears shades even when it's not sunny and doesn't take notes; it doesn't lug around a backpack full of uncool textbooks. Distant cool makes its disdain very clear. As a result, alienated "cool" can attract unfavorable attention from professors and from serious, "uncool," students, which only reinforces an "us-against-them" sense of detachment.

- **Alienated cool's habit of mocking character traits that lead to academic and economic success is a serious stumbling block to learning.** By mocking and ridiculing students who worry about their grades and who participate in class, aloof cool increases the risk of shutting us off from succeeding at anything besides being cool. Being cool by "beating the system" or remaining aloof reinforces a false sense of superiority; false because it doesn't take much ability to cheat teachers with large class loads. And there's a real risk that by adopting the view that education is just one more cynical game, the distantly cool student reinforces an I-don't-give-a-you-know-what mind-set that impedes success in most walks of life.

- **Cool's range of influence is surprisingly limited.** Cool is most appealing to people who have a heightened need for validation from other people. Cool is not very influential in graduate school, at most jobs, when applying for a loan, in court, and so on. It's one thing to be selectively cool, but being defensively or aggressively cool can be self-limiting if it becomes a major life goal.

■ **It's cooler to do well in school than it is to waste a chance at a better future.** If you like being cool, be cool enough to maximize your time in college. If the joys of learning and mastery don't move you, then surely the chance to live a richer life, a life of more choices and opportunities does. And that alone should be a sufficient motive to be a good student. If it is, that's really cool.

4

How to Thrive
in a Philosophy Class

The real reason for failure is unwillingness,
the pretended reason, inability.
SENECA

You've probably had science courses, history classes, English courses, and social science classes in high school. You may even have had a philosophy-type class or two in high school or a philosophical teacher. I hope you did. But even if you did, most college-level philosophy courses have some special features that it's good to know about. This chapter focuses on those special features and on ways to avoid the most common anxieties and pitfalls that plague beginning philosophy students.

The one thing almost every philosophy class has in common is a focus on extended arguments concerning value judgments, truth claims, standards of meaning, the nature of knowledge, reality, social justice, and so forth. As a general rule, philosophical questions cannot be settled by the empirical sciences or appeals to religious faith—although scientific evidence and religious beliefs do play a role in some philosophical speculation. Nor can philosophical questions be settled by simple appeals to personal conviction and experience, to common sense, or by referring to psychological or social causes—although they, too, play important roles in philosophical thinking.

Regardless of the specific format or content of your introductory philosophy courses, you will be encouraged to think for yourself in critical and sophisticated ways. You will be taught to present others' arguments fairly and accurately and required to provide reasons for any position you take on any philosophical topic.

The following passage from the rationalist philosopher **René Descartes' (1596–1650)** *Rules for the Direction of the Mind* reminds us that our beliefs remain shaky and "second hand," not really ours, until we think them through for ourselves:

> For we shall not, e.g., turn out to be mathematicians though we know by heart all the proofs others have elaborated, unless we have an intellectual talent that fits us to resolve difficulties of any kind. Neither, though we may have mastered all the arguments of Plato and Aristotle, if yet we have not the capacity for passing solid judgment on these matters, shall we become Philosophers; we should have acquired the knowledge not of a [philosophy], but of history.

Philosophy instructors want to help you acquire philosophical understanding, not just information or empty technique. Consequently, they are as interested in your learning to ask the right questions as they are in helping you get the right answers. You will not be expected to "solve" or "settle" great philosophical issues, only to understand some basic ones, and to think carefully about them.

Because philosophers themselves disagree about the proper way to philosophize, there are no universally accepted formulae to follow in philosophy courses like there are in math or science courses. Your philosophy instructor may disagree with many things in this book or your textbook—even if he or she is the one who assigned them. That's because philosophers value even flawed arguments and texts if they raise important questions or lead to better thinking. If your school has more than one introductory philosophy teacher, it won't be surprising to find that different teachers have different approaches to the "same course." The next time you're in the campus bookstore, take a look at the texts required for different sections of the same philosophy course.

They will give you some idea of how much variety there can be in one philosophy department.

> I do not know how to teach philosophy without becoming a disturber of the peace.—Baruch Spinoza

However, much they differ, most introductory philosophy courses share a fundamental interest in critical thinking and critical and analytic writing; that is, they place great value on supporting claims with reasons. Most philosophy instructors share a commitment to encouraging you to think for yourself. Because you will be required to respond actively to philosophers' arguments in a rational way, a philosophy class is not the place to be if you are intellectually lazy.

Immanuel Kant used the term "self-imposed tutelage" to characterize a kind of mental laziness that sometimes makes actively thinking for ourselves difficult. Tutelage is a form of slavery or dependency. Kant thought that the process of thinking for ourselves could release us from "self-imposed tutelage." He wrote:

> Tutelage is the inability to use one's natural powers without direction from another. This tutelage is called "self-imposed" because it came about not by any absence of rational competence but simply a lack of courage and resolution to use one's reason without direction from another. *Sapere aude!*— Dare to reason! Have the courage to use your own minds!— is the motto of the enlightenment.
>
> Laziness and cowardice explain why so many . . . remain under a life-long tutelage and why it is so easy for some . . . to set themselves up as the guardians of all the rest. . . . If I have a book which understands for me, a pastor who has a conscience for me, a doctor who decides my diet, I need not trouble myself. If I am willing to pay, I need not think. Others will do it for me.

Your philosophy instructor will almost certainly be an enemy of "self-imposed tutelage." But that doesn't mean that all philosophy teachers are alike. Philosophy teachers vary in the emphasis they put on factual and historical information, but as a rule, philosophy courses do not require learning as many names and dates as a history course might, or as many facts and technical terms as a geography course. Unfortunately, this leads unwary students to overlook the role that accurate information plays in assessing philosophical arguments. It is impossible to consider an issue critically if you do not memorize some basic facts, be they historical, technical, or the meanings of key terms and concepts. Don't be lulled into laxness if your philosophy courses don't involve extensive concentration on facts. You'll still need to learn—and memorize—key facts, figures, terms, and concepts to place "big ideas" in their proper contexts.

The late Charles "Gus" Garrigus, a lifelong educator and former poet laureate of California, used to say that "Memorization furnishes the mind." Garrigus believed, rightly I think, that rote memorization gets a bad rap in educational circles these days. Certainly, mere memorization is no substitute for such refined and desirable abilities as: comprehension, assessment, and speculation. But, as Garrigus taught, it is impossible to "think" without thinking about something. We must furnish our minds with facts, names, dates, terms, definitions, arguments, principles, and standards. The novice welder expects to memorize all sorts of safety procedures, metallurgic properties, temperature effects, and you no doubt expect to memorize facts and new terms in biology and Spanish classes. Approach philosophy with the same expectation—and willingness—to memorize technical philosophical terms, complex arguments, and, where relevant, historical dates and context.

Academic excellence begins with a solid foundation of information for each subject you study, usually beginning with terminology and then progressing from information to comprehension and mastery.

In one way or another, virtually all of the world's traditions teach that, for most of us, knowledge and wisdom do not come without some struggle and disappointment. Learning how to learn is no exception. There is no "painless" way to become a good student—but, then, there is no painless way to become a good child, parent, athlete, or friend.

ACQUIRING INFORMED OPINIONS

Although you already probably have opinions about many of the topics covered in philosophy courses, you may not have had the opportunity to analyze and justify these opinions in the sustained, critical way that will be expected of you in a philosophy class. You will be expected to give and justify your own informed opinions about philosophical concepts.

Unfortunately, this emphasis on the give-and-take of competing opinions has led to the common misconception that philosophy is "just one philosopher's opinion versus another philosopher's opinion." Even if this is true—and to a large extent it is—philosophy is not *just* a matter of opinion. The idea that it is rests on the naïve notion that one belief is as good as another.

"Mere" beliefs are convictions grounded solely on the sincerity of the believer that they are true. Even when they are true, mere beliefs are unanchored. They rely on psychological conviction instead of informed arguments and fact-based evidence. As such, they tell us something about the believer but almost nothing about the belief. **Unvetted opinions** are a tiny, inadequate, step up from mere beliefs. Unvetted opinions are convictions based on vague notions, common prejudices, and such sources as the mass media and partisan individuals speaking out on issues that they have not subjected to sustained, organized, critical study.

You cannot judge by annoyance—Idries Shah

Sadly, today's sound-bite, media-driven popular culture can be hostile to informed, carefully assessed and presented opinions. Providing solid, balanced justification for our opinions doesn't make good "sound bites" on the evening news. Television and radio talk shows inundate us with shouting, belligerent, sincere, or at least sincere-sounding, advocates for all sorts of positions. What they rarely provide—or even tolerate—is the time and care necessary for thoughtful reflection and analysis of even the most important issues. Throw in those big, hokey roundtable discussions and instant, come-one-come-all Internet polls regarding technical matters, and it's no wonder we confuse the expression of a mere belief with a justification for believing it. I sometimes suspect that most talk show hosts, advertisers, politicians, and committed social reformers don't want us to think for ourselves as much as they want us to agree with them and to support their causes or buy their products.

SPECIAL FEATURES
OF PHILOSOPHY COURSES

Your philosophy instructor will encourage you to develop thinking skills to resist self-imposed and media-imposed tutelage. Thinking for yourself is like accomplishing anything for yourself—it may be more difficult than letting someone else do things for you, but it's also much more satisfying and liberating. It's satisfying because skills mastery is intrinsically pleasing, and it's liberating in the practical realm because you are in the driver's seat when you think for yourself.

Expect your philosophy instructor to demand that you present reasons to support your opinions, and that you do so with rigor and clarity. Your instructor is there to show you how to meet high standards of proof, not to show up your faults or attack your personal beliefs. The only way to learn how to present good reasons is by recognizing bad—or nonexistent—ones, especially when they're your own. Fear of being wrong is always a stumbling block to learning. That's too bad, because an error that's corrected is no longer an error, whereas an error that's unacknowledged remains an error.

A common method of teaching philosophy involves deliberately challenging your present beliefs—not because they are necessarily insupportable, but to help you see just how sound or unsound they are. Although it can be discouraging to discover that you can't support some of your most cherished beliefs, it's worth the discomfort to discover how often you can. In either event, your philosophy instructor is likely to be more concerned with helping you learn how to think philosophically than with teaching you what to think. This process can be frustrating if you are used to being told "the truth" by authority figures or if you don't have much tolerance for ambiguity.

The combination of sometimes controversial, often abstract topics, and the introduction of new standards of proof can confuse new philosophy students. Stick with it. Work at refining your thinking skills and initial frustration will turn to interest and possibly even enchantment. You'll take justifiable pride in your more polished thinking. Once you experience the intellectual thrill—and it really is a thrill—that comes from challenging important ideas according to rigorous standards, you'll never want to settle for less. Here are some of the best things about philosophy courses:

- Philosophy courses devote considerable attention to reasons and arguments. Precision and clarity are highly valued.

- Students—and instructors—are expected to defend interpretations and positions rationally.

- Many philosophical arguments are complex and abstract.

- There are often equally compelling reasons supporting conflicting points of view.

- The topics studied in philosophy courses often challenge or directly reject commonly held opinions.

- Most philosophy instructors place as much, if not more, emphasis on the reasoning offered for a position as they do on "getting the right answer."

- Many, if not most, of the philosophies covered in your course will seem persuasive and flawed at the same time. (That's because they are.)

- Philosophy has been characterized as the art of questioning and although this can be frustrating to students used to getting "the correct answer," philosophical questioning quickly proves exhilarating to most students.

- No philosophical idea or value is sacred. Any philosophical position worth holding is a fair subject for critical analysis.

GETTING THE MOST OUT
OF A PHILOSOPHY (OR ANY) CLASS

- **Develop a mature attitude.** Give all ideas a fair initial hearing, even if you can't imagine holding them yourself. Don't "shoot from the hip" and make impulsive, uninformed prejudgments.

- **Participate in class.** Volunteer to answer questions when the instructor asks them. Offer supporting examples. Ask for clarification.

- **Don't confuse having a strong opinion with being right.** You probably hold strong beliefs about many issues you've not recently (if ever) thoroughly and objectively studied.

- **Don't immediately express your objections to new ideas.** Make sure you understand the entire issue and its significance to the point being developed in class before raising objections. If you find yourself repeatedly tempted to object to "wrong" beliefs, you may be locked into a defensive attitude that will prevent you from understanding many of the things you are expected to learn. Don't try to get a good education (especially a philosophical one) and also retain all of your present ideas. You will not have gotten much of an education if you are the same person at graduation that you were when you began college.

- **Practice the principle of charity.** In simple terms, the principle of charity directs you to begin your analysis of a passage or argument by interpreting any ambiguities and apparent inconsistencies to the advantage of the point being advanced. This will prevent you from reading with a selective bias or prejudice against a position that challenges a cherished belief or that expresses a new idea. Your first careful reading of a philosophical passage should always be based on the assumption that the author's intention is to present good reasons for his or her position—and that he or she is capable of doing so. This attitude gives you the best chance of understanding the original argument. It minimizes the chances that you will distort ideas that you don't like. Psychologists who study learning report that people have the most difficulty understanding and remembering ideas with which they disagree. Use that insight to help you become a better student and better thinker by consciously resisting the impulse to look for weaknesses before you fully grasp a position. (DO NOT EXPECT YOUR PROFESSOR TO READ YOUR COURSE WORK UNDER THE PRINCIPLE OF CHARITY. YOUR INSTRUCTOR WILL MOST LIKELY INTERPRET GAPS, INCONSISTENCIES, AND AMBIGUITIES AS ERRORS ON YOUR PART AS A WAY OF HOLDING YOU TO HIGH STANDARDS. TO DO ANYTHING LESS WOULD BE DISRESPECTFUL TO YOU.)

- **Think in terms of understanding rather than judging.**

- **Continually ask yourself why you believe X and not Y.**

- **Don't settle for superficial, easy answers.**

- **Work, work, work.** Accept the fact that to understand what's going on in class you'll need to read your assignments on time, and most likely need to reread them once or twice.

- **Write while you read.** There is no substitute for carefully reading all assignments. The more you read, the better you read. "Reading" involves more than just following words on a page. Reading—real reading—involves studying what is said, thinking it over, assessing it.

Taking notes as you read is an excellent way to improve reading comprehension. (And your notes will come in handy when it is time to review for tests or prepare essays.)

- **Come to class with informed questions—and ask them.**

- **If a point made in class is unclear, wait a few minutes to see whether subsequent remarks clear it up.** If not, ask for clarification. If you cannot bring yourself to ask questions during class, make a specific note of your confusion. After class, write your question neatly, and give it to your instructor before the next class meeting. Meanwhile, study the issue on your own, and, if necessary, modify your notes.

- **Ask for clarification of all assignments when they are made.** Don't ever leave class without being very sure you understand all assignments.

- **Follow instructions.** Don't make any modification without specific—explicit—permission from your instructor.

- **Find a "study buddy."** Make arrangements with another class member to study outside of class and to share notes and information when one of you has missed a class.

- **Always take your book to class.** You never know when it will come in handy.

- **Sit up front, toward the center.** Studies indicate that where you sit can affect your performance in class. If you sit near the instructor, you'll feel more involved in class. It's more difficult to daydream and doze off right under the professor's nose. From a statistical point of view, the most academically dangerous seats are those that create a sense of distance and anonymity—far back, rear sides, and the obscure middle of large lecture halls.

DECIDING WHAT IS NOTEWORTHY

- **Always come to class prepared to take notes.** You'll certainly want to record assignment due dates and changes in the schedule in your notes.

- **Be spacious.** Take plenty of paper to class so that you can leave plenty of space between key words and phrases in your initial notes. If you use lined paper, skip two or three lines between each distinct idea, argument, issue, term, and so forth. When you review your notes, you can add clarifying details from the textbook, dictionaries, and study sessions with other students. You may find it helpful to make two columns for notes, one for basic lecture information and the other to be used when adding clarifying details later.

- **For lectures that repeat the text.** Some instructors prefer to follow the text closely in their lectures. In that case, you won't need to take very thorough notes regarding the *information* conveyed in class. You'll probably do best by *not* trying to write down every name, date, definition, and idea mentioned in class (you can look them up in the text). Instead, listen carefully for new insights or alternative explanations of complex ideas, making note of them by using key phrases that will remind you of helpful examples, analogies, and simplified definitions when you review and flesh out your notes later (as you, of course, will do).

- **For lectures that convey information not found in the text.** If your instructor's lectures contain a wealth of new information, you will need to take careful, thorough notes. You might consider developing your own form of shorthand. If you do, be consistent. For example, many people use w/ to mean "with" and @ to mean "according to."

- **For lectures that consist of wide-ranging elaborations on key ideas, but do not repeat or strictly follow the text.** Don't attempt to record such lectures verbatim, and don't attempt to organize their content as you take notes. Some of the best lecturers are the most difficult to take notes from because their lectures have a life of their own. No two lectures on Socrates, for instance, are ever the same for some spellbinding master lecturers. Don't be frustrated. Relax and "go with the flow."

- **You cannot (and need not) take exhaustive, conventional notes from philosophical lecturers.** Your instructor probably expects you to get detailed information from the text and, rather than "lecture," uses class time to demonstrate how philosophers "do philosophy."

- **Record all new and/or complex information and ideas.** Don't assume that you'll be able to remember everything you hear in class. There may simply be too many new ideas for that to be possible. Further, you will need time to distill new ideas. Take notes that will enable you to concentrate on relationships and connections among ideas. Copy all alternative definitions and explanations for technical philosophical terms. Record illustrative examples.

- **Don't try to take notes word for word.** Jot down key words and phrases, make diagrams.

- **Record all charts, definitions, and outlines from the board or overhead projections (if they are not from the text).**

▪ **Take special care to RECORD EVERY IDEA YOU DISLIKE.** Cognitive scientists have shown that we tend to overlook, forget, or distort ideas that challenge or seriously disagree with our most cherished desires and fundamental beliefs. This is known as confirmation bias. The social psychologist Carol Tavris describes confirmation bias as the "most entrenched human cognitive habit." If we are not alert, we trivialize and unconsciously alter opposing ideas to make them less threatening. Unpleasant and threatening ideas are also more difficult to understand, so you'll need to put special effort into recording them accurately and completely—and into studying them later.

▪ **Be very careful to include all modifiers and qualifying terms.** Words like "always," "sometimes," "probably," "might," "never," and the like are crucial parts of claims. Leaving them out significantly changes the meaning of the original idea. Example: Changing "philosophy and religion sometimes overlap" to "philosophy and religion overlap" alters the meaning of the original sentence.

▪ **Ask questions and make comments as part of your notes.** Jot down questions and strong reactions you have to ideas expressed in class. Use a "?" to mean "why?" Be brief but clear. "Proof?" can mean "How does X know? What's the evidence?" "!" can mean "great!" or "wow!" Use "N" for "no" and "Y" for "yes" to indicate disagreement or agreement. Use "NB" from the Latin *nota bene* for "note well" (pay attention).

▪ **Polish your notes soon after you take them.** Go over your notes the same day you make them. Try to make a quick polish within an hour or so after you've taken your notes. Fill in details. Restate cloudy passages. Use the generous spaces you left to amplify your necessarily incomplete notes.

▪ **Don't reduce your instructor to a talking textbook.** You have a textbook to use as a textbook. Think of your instructor as a valuable source of enrichment, clarification, guidance, and support. To get the most out of class, don't treat class time as study hall and don't treat lectures as substitutes for careful reading.

WHY ATTENDANCE MATTERS

▪ **Studies consistently confirm that poor attendance is highly coordinated with poor academic performance and low levels of satisfaction.** For instance, a 2000 study found that students who attended class 95% of the time had an 85% pass rate on a tough statewide language-arts test. The 2004 National Survey of Student Engagement (NSSE) confirmed a positive correlation between college success (good grades and personal satisfaction) and regular class attendance. If that sounds like common sense, that's because it is.

- **In addition to being a set of key issues and individuals, philosophy is a skill and a way of thinking that contributes to "deep learning."** Deep learning is closely correlated with effective use of time and doing well academically and personally (NSSE 2004). You need to experience the way your instructor "does philosophy" on a regular basis if you want to do more than just acquire philosophical information.

- **You're more likely to learn if you feel safe and comfortable when you know what's going on.** Instructors often modify schedules, announce extensions for assignments, and so forth, in class. You want to get this useful information right away.

- **Getting to know and recognize classmates, no matter how casually, will enhance your sense of belonging.** You'll be more comfortable and hence more likely to discuss course material and share common frustrations before and after class if you're on friendly terms with other students. Every little bit of anxiety reduction helps.

- **Attending class regularly keeps philosophical issues at the forefront of your mind.** Not all learning is deliberate and conscious. Listening to your instructor's explanations and elaborations of textual material can trigger new connections for you (deep learning), can spark your own creative ideas, and can identify areas of misunderstanding.

- **When an instructor says that "attendance does not count," this only refers to his or her formal grading policy.** Attendance always affects your learning. Assigning grades is a complex process and it is reasonable for your instructor to wonder if you have learned in-class material covered during your absences, and not award the higher of two possible grades if you've been absent frequently.

- **Regular feedback from students helps teachers be better teachers.** Most instructors modify their courses according to student comments and questions. They are vital clues for gearing a course's content and pace to its audience.

RELATING TO YOUR PROFESSOR

Your philosophy professor wants you to succeed by acquiring new knowledge, learning important facts and terms, polishing your critical thinking skills, discovering new facets of yourself, and experiencing the many pleasures of the mind. And he or she wants you to accomplish this in a way that's congenial to both of you.

Just as it is to your advantage to have a competent, courteous, friendly, professional professor, it is to your professor's advantage to have eager, inquisitive, hardworking, and courteous students. It's helpful to keep that in mind when you interact with your professor, especially when you are discouraged and frustrated. Here are tips and guidelines for making the most of your interactions with your professors and teachers.

> According to the most recent National Survey of Student Engagement, 40% of first-year students and 25% of seniors "never" discuss ideas from their classes or readings with a faculty member outside of class. What a loss—to faculty as well as those students.

- **Always respect your teacher's role and position, regardless of your feelings about the person.** If you have the unfortunate experience of being stuck with a teacher you find difficult or ineffective, remind yourself that in spite of his or her weaknesses, this teacher has probably completed several years of higher education. At the very least, he or she is entitled to the respect due the position of teacher.

- **Communicate, communicate, communicate.** Your professor cannot read your mind. It is your responsibility to let him or her know when something is not clear, or whenever you have a special concern. Since you are responsible for all assignments, it is important to understand exactly what is expected.

- **Study the course syllabus as soon as you receive it.** Learn what is important to your instructor. Learn the location of his or her office, designated office hours, and office phone number.

- **Address your instructor the way he or she prefers.** Some instructors prefer to be addressed as Mr., Mrs., or Ms., others as Doctor or Professor. Simple courtesy and pragmatism suggest that you do as requested. Although some instructors prefer to be addressed by their first names, do not use an instructor's first name until invited to do so.

- **Request, don't demand.** The Taoists teach (correctly, I think) that "Forceful actions rebound." This means that aggression breeds aggression, attack breeds counterattack. No matter how nervous, frightened, or angry you are, try not to approach your instructor in a rude, belligerent, demanding, or sarcastic manner. Doing so may pollute the interaction before it begins. Instructors can be just as insecure as you are. When attacked, some of them immediately become defensive and resistant to your message.

- **Speak for yourself.** As a rule, it is illegal for your professor to discuss your grades or class work with anyone but you. Unless seriously injured or incarcerated, do not ask parents, friends, coaches, or other instructors to speak for you to your instructor. You are, after all, a college student.

- **Stay in touch.** If you have to miss a few classes or cannot meet an assignment deadline, ask your instructor if you can make up missed work. Do not just assume that you will or won't be allowed an extension.

- **Think about how you say things.** Most instructors do not appreciate remarks such as: "I missed class Tuesday. Did we do anything important?" or "That's dumb. Why'd we waste class time on it?" Consider these more effective alternatives: "I'm sorry I was not in class Tuesday. What can I study to help make up for what I missed?" "I'm not clear as to the significance of this material. Could you explain it further for me?" If you hate philosophy, there's no particular reason to volunteer that fact to the person who's devoted a lifetime to it.

- **Don't flirt with or date your instructor. Period.** Even if you believe that your personal involvement with your instructor has no bearing on your grades, other students won't believe that. And they will find out about your involvement. If you break up with your instructor, you may find yourself in the awkward position of being graded by your "ex."

- **Don't tolerate sexual harassment.** If your instructor flirts with you, makes inappropriate personal comments, or somehow makes you uncomfortable in a sexual way, you are in a delicate spot. Tell your instructor you are not comfortable. If that does not take care of the problem, talk to the instructor's immediate supervisor.

- **Let your instructor know what works and what doesn't.** Instructors get less useful feedback about their courses than you might guess. Vague compliments or criticisms ("Great class!" or "Boy, was that boring!") don't help us develop and retain good features and modify, or delete, bad ones. Be specific when commenting on what works or doesn't work.

- **Share your enthusiasm.** Perhaps nothing delights a teacher more than expressions of interest in a course. Ask for additional works by a favorite philosopher. Stop by and tell your instructor about a connection you've made between something from philosophy class and another class, or that has some special relevance to your daily life.

■ **Avoid appeals to pity.** If you have a special request, make it in as straightforward a way as possible. Avoid committing the logical fallacy known as *appeal to pity.* An appeal to pity occurs when a person attempts to advance a conclusion by evoking feelings of pity in others, when pity is irrelevant to the matter at hand. If you have special circumstances that interfere with getting an assignment in on time or taking a test, you should certainly inform your instructor in a timely way. If, however, you anticipate having to request exemptions and extensions on a regular basis, you should probably take the course at some other time. Appealing to pity can be risky, too; you won't know if it will move your professor to help you or to treat you as an excuse-maker or whiner. Note, too, that self-respect is incompatible with appeals to pity. If you have legitimate reasons to ask for special help, ask for help, not pity.

■ **When you just cannot get along with your teacher, take appropriate, informed action on your own behalf.** Your remedies will range from talking things over with the teacher to going to the department head or a higher-level administrator in very serious situations. If the problem is a personality or teaching-style clash, you may have to choose between evils: sticking it out and doing your best, or dropping the class and taking it later from a different instructor. When in doubt, consult with a trusted counselor or other knowledgeable individual as soon as you suspect that ordinary solutions won't work.

CONFERENCES WITH YOUR PROFESSOR

■ **Always introduce yourself.** Until you're sure that your instructor knows your name, always introduce yourself and identify the particular course section you attend.

■ **Make a good faith effort to meet during scheduled office hours.** You don't want to waste your instructor's time, or give the impression that you are irresponsible. So don't be irresponsible.

■ **Be on time.** Politely, let your professor know you have arrived.

■ **Keep your appointments, or notify the instructor or the department secretary if you cannot.** This simple courtesy is also pragmatic: It keeps you on good terms with your professor. Keep track of appointments, and if you miss one, contact your instructor as soon as possible. Whatever your reason for missing the appointment—even if it's just forgetting—don't simply avoid mentioning it. If you don't have a good excuse, apologize; if you have an excuse, use it. The worst thing to do when you have any kind of problem with a class is nothing. Your philosophy instructor wants to help you succeed and will work with you if you make a solid effort—and if you communicate.

- **Knock before opening a closed office door.** If your professor's office door is closed, don't just open it. Knock and wait for a reply.

- **If there is something you have a particular problem with, write out your problem clearly and specifically before going to your professor.** Often, the very act of formulating a clear question or statement regarding a problem will make the answer clear to you—or point you to the answer. Your statement will still be a great help to your professor, making it easier for him or her to help you. It's easy to forget even the most important things during a discussion. If you have a written list, you can make sure that you've covered everything that's important to you.

- **If you are discussing a grade on a test or paper, always bring the graded test or paper with you.** Don't expect your instructor to remember the details of every test or paper. Give your instructor time to review the graded material before launching into questions or complaints.

- **Cool off before you discuss something that's really bothering you.** Don't rush right over and complain about a test or paper grade based on your first reaction. Wait at least one day. Carefully reassess the issue. If it continues to be important to you, consult your instructor.

Remember, you are working for yourself. You have doubtless heard, "I have a theme to write for__. I have thirty pages to read for__. I have ten pages to write for old__." Nothing could be further from the truth. You do a lot of work in school, but none of it is done for the teacher. You are working to develop not the teacher but yourself.—William H. Armstrong

---

5

Reading Philosophy

If you do not read good books you have no advantage
over the person who cannot read them.
MARK TWAIN

Most philosophical literature attempts to make a rational case that supports a clearly articulated point of view. As a rule, even when philosophical literature is emotionally powerful, creative, and witty, these nonrational qualities take second place to the philosophical argument.

More often than not, philosophers attempt to construct tightly reasoned chains of ideas leading from basic, initially clear, ideas to less obvious, more complex ones. As a consequence of this rigor, reading philosophical literature requires patience and concentration. Because key points are connected to earlier key points, it's just as important not to lose track of the line of reasoning as it is to understand the overall point of the passage. This can't always be done in a single reading.

Philosophers often invent their own technical vocabulary in an attempt to be both clear and fair. Sometimes philosophers coin brand new words; other times they give their own special meanings to words already in use. Failure to note the precise meaning of key terms results in failure to follow the philosopher's line of reasoning. Having to keep track of technical philosophical meanings can be difficult, but it cannot be avoided.

Not all philosophers are careful to define the unique meanings of key terms, so careful philosophical readers are always on the lookout for unusual uses of common terms as well as for newly coined terms. Sometimes, philosophers even use the same technical term to mean different things—without warning the reader. So in addition to watching for the meaning of key terms, always check to see that terms retain a consistent meaning.

Don't be surprised if your first reading of a philosophical text confuses you. I find that I must often read new philosophical arguments at least twice, and often three times before I completely understand all of their implications and nuances. This is true even with texts I've read before, especially if it's been a while since I have studied them.

When you find yourself confused and frustrated, remember that you are learning a new philosophical vocabulary as well as trying to identify a line of reasoning that may involve sidelines and subpoints. This requires a form of mental juggling that involves retaining a variety of isolated pieces of information until you can identify the overall structure of the argument. (The overall structure of an argument is not the same thing as its point or conclusion.)

Don't be intimidated or surprised if you sometimes—or even often—find yourself confused by a philosophical argument. Most of that confusion clears up if you merely persist by being as attentive as possible at each reading. With persistence, you will find that after a few more pages of close reading, your comprehension suddenly improves. When that happens, it's a good idea to go back and immediately reread the material that confused you. You'll be surprised at how much clearer it is.

> It matters, if individuals are to retain any capacity to form their own judgments and opinions, that they continue to read for themselves.
> —Harold Bloom

Critical reading skills can be learned and refined by just about anyone who is willing to work at it. When it comes to figuring out what accounts for college success, motivation and effort are at least as important as natural ability. Critical reading skills can be developed by regular, focused work. Philosophical literature, like most technical writing, poses special problems that can be greatly reduced by the application of some basic principles of effective critical reading. Effective readers take advantage of a variety of clues and strategies that simplify the process of understanding and evaluating different kinds of writing. They also read regularly. No matter how difficult a subject is for you, spending as much time reading philosophy (or history or botany) as you might spend reading about sports, movies, or fashions will eventually make reading philosophy (or history or botany)—and anything else—easier.

Fortunately, you don't have to just "tough it out" and slog away without any finesse and hope that everything suddenly makes sense. Philosophers and reading experts have identified a number of strategies and tips to help you get the most out of your textbooks and other assigned readings. I've included some here, beginning with a list that reminds us to get to know our books before we begin to study them.

USE YOUR TEXTBOOKS'
ORGANIZATIONAL FEATURES

- **Always read the preface.** Reading the preface is like having a chat with the author of your textbook. The preface usually includes a brief description of the book's special features and why the author thinks they will help readers. Reading the preface will familiarize you with the author's "voice," the special style he or she has. Lastly, the preface may identify the author's chief goals and philosophical principles.

- **Get to know your textbook right away.** Read the entire table of contents. Read one or two brief passages that catch your interest. Familiarize yourself with any special features designed to make the book more accessible, interesting, or understandable: appendices, margin quotations, boxed passages, illustrations, summaries of main points, and study questions.

- **Use the index.** One of the best ways to understand new concepts is to see how they apply in different contexts. A good index can alert the reader to the use of key terms in different chapters. The best indexes categorize terms under subheadings and outline relationships via cross-references. Indexes are invaluable research tools. (Note: Some books have more than one index.)

- **Take full advantage of margin quotes, boxed text, or offset passages.** Such features will have been carefully selected because they are especially interesting, well written, or unusual. Don't skip by them, enjoy them.

- **Familiarize yourself with the glossary (a list of definitions of key terms).** The glossary can be at the end of the text, at the beginning or end of chapters or sections, in the margins, or in some combination. Some books have more than one glossary.

- **Study section headings.** They tell you how the author has organized the text and provide clues about its content. Section headings are like levels in an outline. In addition to labeling text sections, they classify and categorize them.

- **Before you read a chapter, review the table of contents for that chapter.** If your textbook has a detailed table of contents, it will show the various levels of headings and subheadings in each chapter. Treat them like an outline. Knowing the structure of a chapter will aid in understanding its content.

- **Use section headings to organize your notes.** Some students find it helpful to list the chapter headings on sheets of notepaper, allowing lots of room between headings. This provides a structure for lecture or reading notes. You can always modify notes by adding organizational categories. The point—to repeat—is to be an active reader and note taker.

- **Take full advantage of chapter summaries and study questions.** Read summaries and study questions early in your study of a chapter. They flag important concepts that you need to understand—and that are likely to turn up on tests.

- **Use self-sticking notes to flag every passage you find difficult.** If a passage remains unclear after careful rereading, ask your instructor to go over it with you.

- **Take your text to class regularly so that you can follow along with the instructor if he or she refers to it.**

THE VIRTUES OF ANNOTATING
YOUR OWN TEXT

Annotations are notes and comments written in the margins of a text by a reader. Annotating a text discourages passive reading; it is like a conversation conducted in writing. If you have ever looked through a book that's been annotated, you know how personal and interesting annotations can be. Looking through a book that has been annotated by someone else is almost like observing another person's thinking process. Though some people find it difficult to write in their books, annotating a text can be a valuable study aid. Of course it ought to go without saying that you shouldn't annotate a text that you don't own.

The very act of annotating a text requires you to respond to what you're reading: to inquire, praise, criticize, or to express delight or astonishment. By annotating, you create your own handy reference notes to use in class, when reviewing for tests, or when researching for essays and term papers.

- **Be selective.** Don't underline too much—or too little—or you'll find yourself annoyed when it's time to reread indiscriminately annotated sections and discouraged when you're looking through vaguely annotated passages.

- **Be critical, in a simple way.** Note "Yes," "No," or even "B.S." or "Wow!"—anything that works to get you involved in a dialogue with the text can help you better understand what you're reading.

- **If at all possible, buy your books with money you have earned or have borrowed (and will repay with money you earn).** Spending your own money on textbooks reinforces your commitment to success in college.

- **What if you can't afford to purchase your own books?** Most colleges have financial aid and short-term emergency loans available for students who cannot afford to buy necessary supplies. Taking the time and effort to secure financial aid or loans is another way of reinforcing your commitment to success in a class.

- **Won't annotating a text diminish its resale value?** It probably will. But you have to decide how important succeeding in a particular class (and in college in general) is to you. If your only choice is between reselling your books and eating or dropping out of college, then perhaps you should not write in your books. But if you somehow can afford to rent videos, go to concerts, buy cokes and beer, order a pizza, buy

DVDs, and so forth, then you can afford to annotate your text—by giving up some of these luxuries for a time.

QUICK TIPS FOR READING PHILOSOPHY (AND ANYTHING ELSE)

- **Suspend personal judgments and don't forget the principle of charity (see Chapter 4).** Completely ignore whether or not you like what is being argued. Your initial readings should be only for comprehension. Evaluation should come later because critical evaluation depends on first understanding what is being claimed and how well that claim is supported. If you don't do this, you'll end up confusing your own fantasy notion of a philosopher's ideas with the real thing.

- **Always skim to get an overview.** Skim the table of contents of the book (or the headings in a chapter). Flip through articles, chapters, or sections using headings and subheadings to get a sense of organizational structure. Read the preface or introductory notes provided by the editor or author. Check to see if there is an index or an appendix and if there is, use it. See if there's a glossary of technical terms; if there is, use it early and use it often.

- **Read to get the general idea of a passage's main point and a sense of its strategy for establishing that point in mind.** You can get this information from chapter summaries, from your instructor, and from other books and articles. (See the Beginning Philosopher's Bibliography at the end of this book for a list of some good supplemental philosophy sources.)

- **Read with a pencil, highlighter, or pad of self-sticking notes handy, and flag technical philosophical terms and important passages as you come across them.**

- **Read in good light.**

- **Find a comfortable spot away from distractions.** Some people study better with a little background music, others don't. Do what works for you. Pick a study spot that's good for your needs—and whenever possible always study in the same spot.

- **Make reading a priority.** If you become distracted by thoughts of other things you need to do, write them down to deal with after you are through reading. Then, tell yourself that this is your time to read. Stay focused on reading.

■ **Use the glossary and a good unabridged dictionary. Look up difficult words right away.** Every serious reader, to say nothing of every serious college student, ought to own a dictionary—and keep it handy.

■ **Consider buying a specialized philosophy dictionary.** General reference dictionaries cannot be relied on for technical definitions of philosophical terms. I've recommended some superb philosophy dictionaries in the Beginning Philosopher's Bibliography. If you don't want to buy your own, see if your college's library has one or two. If it does not, ask the reference librarian to purchase one for the school library.

■ **Read through an entire section in one sitting, even if you don't understand most of it.** After your first reading, you'll have a clearer idea of the structure of the argument or explanation. You'll be in good shape to reread more closely. You'll understand much more on the second reading because you will know how points made in one part of the passage relate to points made elsewhere. You'll also know what's most important, and why.

■ **Take regular breaks that are long enough to clear your mind and give your eyes a rest.** Stop reading often enough to prevent fatigue. Don't consciously think about what you've just read. Move around, stretch. Let your unconscious mind process the material.

■ **Reread as often as you need to.** Don't fall into the trap of comparing your study needs to others' study needs.

■ **Vary your reading speed.** As a general rule, you need to read important, technically difficult passages at a slower rate than less complex informational passages.

■ **Pause regularly to see if you can clearly restate difficult passages in your own words.** Don't just assume that you understand something because you're not having any noticeable trouble reading it. Forcing yourself to restate important ideas at regular intervals is an effective way of testing comprehension.

■ **Reread difficult passages in a different way.** You may find that you have to take one sentence at a time when reading especially complex or poorly written technical passages. You may need to look up the meanings of two or three words in one paragraph. Whatever you do, don't merely repeat the kind of reading that's not working.

■ **When you're in a rut, flag and skip unusually difficult passages; return to them later.** Don't spend so much time and effort on one difficult passage that you get completely confused, frustrated, and dispirited. If careful rereading isn't working, continue with the rest of the chapter. This simple strategy may be all you need to clarify the difficult passage.

■ **Ask your instructor to recommend some supplementary reading for especially difficult passages.** If the preceding tips don't seem to be working, consult another text or textbook that deals with the same point. There should be some in the college library; just be sure to check with your instructor if they conflict with your assigned texts. Sometimes just reading a different explanation will clear things right up.

■ **Don't confuse a tired mind or body with reading difficulties.** If nothing you're reading makes sense, or you encounter an especially difficult passage at the end of a long day or study session, you may just be too tired to benefit from more work. Get some rest.

■ **Perform routine maintenance.** Don't get too hungry, thirsty, or tired. Avoid all alcohol and illegal drugs because drugs and alcohol inhibit comprehension skills.

■ **If you are still confused after you've given all these tips a fair try, ask your instructor for additional help.** Sometimes one more clarification or explanation is all it takes to unlock the meaning of a difficult passage.

■ **Make sure you don't have a reading or comprehension problem.** If you are having reading difficulties in most of your classes, consult a counselor. There are simple, free tests your school can provide that can identify common, manageable reading and comprehension difficulties.

■ **If your counselor or instructor recommends the college reading lab, take advantage of its tutorial services.** Don't be too embarrassed to get help if you need it. The folks at the reading lab are there to help you succeed on your own. They will not embarrass you or make you dependent on them. Think of them like physical conditioning coaches: You will do all the work and earn all the credit; they will help you develop better skills.

WHAT TO DO IF NOTHING
SEEMS TO WORK

If you find it impossible to understand assigned readings after carefully following the steps discussed here, you should consult your instructor and, probably, a counselor. You may discover that you need special classes in reading before you can succeed in philosophy. Take advantage of reading tests, reading labs, and related programs, if you need them.

Weak reading skills will not mysteriously disappear. Besides feeling frustrated and depressed because you cannot do as well as you want to, weak reading skills often result in low grades and serious long-term consequences. Don't ignore a reading problem. Confront it as soon as you suspect its presence. Many times, special classes can quickly boost your performance. A wide variety of special programs are available for students with reading and learning difficulties.

BEYOND THE TEXTBOOK

Although your textbook is probably your primary source of detailed subject matter information, it does not have to be your only source. Develop the habit of taking full advantage of all appropriate resources. Become a study artisan using a full set of special tools.

■ **Use this book!** Hang on to *How to Get the Most Out of Philosophy* and review it when you need a study pep talk or a little friendly encouragement.

■ **Maximize your use of your philosophy textbook.** Use all of its pedagogical (teaching and learning) features: chapter introductions, summaries, study questions, glossaries, index, chapter headings, and so forth.

■ **Take advantage of any study guides, student manuals, CD-ROMs, or computerized aids available for your textbook or prepared and distributed by your instructor.** Don't be too "hip" or "cool" to use these features. Among their advantages, four stand out: (1) They focus your attention on key ideas, figures, and so forth. (2) They require active reading. (3) They involve repetition. (4) The best study guides involve active responses.

■ **Regularly check your comprehension by writing down your own summary of a section's key points and arguments in your own words.** Check your summary against the text. If you can accurately and thoroughly summarize a position, you understand it. If you cannot accurately and thoroughly summarize a position, you do not understand it. Period. This is the best self-test you can perform for comprehension. It's important because, as you know, you cannot analyze or evaluate an idea until you can understand it without distorting it.

- **Ask your friends to grade your summaries (see preceding tip), and offer to grade theirs.** This exercise is another opportunity for active reading and thinking. It develops concentration and comprehension.

- **Discuss the philosophical ideas you've been studying.** One of the best ways of testing comprehension is by refining your understanding of an idea or argument by verbally expressing it in your own words to someone else. Better yet, the chance to have regular philosophical discussions with a variety of people is one of the great joys of going to college.

- **Use the library.** Most college libraries have copies of the *Encyclopedia of Philosophy* and a variety of philosophical history books and commentaries, as well as other philosophy textbooks. Ask your instructor to recommend supplemental reading. It's also a good idea just to browse through the philosophy stacks (section of shelves). If you try reading two or three different authors' treatments of the same issues, you'll probably find they're each especially helpful in different ways.

- **Consult reference and technical sources.** See the Beginning Philosopher's Bibliography at the back of this book and the bibliography of your textbook for the names of good reference books. Talk to your college library's reference librarian about in-house and online resources available to students.

- **Take advantage of online resources.** The Internet provides a rich variety of websites maintained by philosophy departments and professors. I've listed a number of them in the Beginning Philosopher's Bibliography. Many colleges subscribe to a variety of Internet portals to large databases unavailable to the general public. Take advantage of these "deep resources."

6

Developing
a Critical Attitude

The student who ignores rules and definitions is all
too soon overcome by ideas that cannot be understood.
WILLIAM H. ARMSTRONG

A critical attitude is one of the most valuable products of a good
education. In this context, "critical" does not mean negative or
hostile. From the Greek root *kritikes*, meaning "to judge" or "to dis-
cern," a critical attitude is one that does not take things at face value,
and that demands reasonable proof before accepting or rejecting claims.

Developing a healthy critical attitude is an especially important
part of any philosophy course. Your philosophy teachers will express
their own critical reactions to philosophical arguments and texts and
they will expect you to do the same. This can be frustrating at first,
especially if you have not had much formal practice analyzing and jus-
tifying your opinions by making sophisticated rational cases for them.
Don't be discouraged. No matter how rough (or how polished) your
critical skills are at the moment, they can be refined and strengthened
like any other skill.

You're probably already familiar with the term "critical thinking."
It is widely used in educational circles. Unfortunately, it's not always

defined clearly, nor is it always used to mean the same thing. Here is a list of some of the chief characteristics of critical thinking as understood by most philosophers:

- **Critical thinking is the conscious and deliberate assessment of claims according to clearly identified standards of proof.** Although appropriate standards of proof vary depending on the nature of the claim, certain fundamental principles of reasoning apply to all critical thinking. These include standards of relevance, consistency, reasonableness (likeliness to be true), and sufficiency. Any claim that rests on inconsistent evidence, inconsistencies between premises and their conclusions, circularity, or ambiguity must be recast or rejected.

- **Critical thinking is objective and impersonal, while recognizing that personal experience and emotion play a part in the thoughtful assessment of claims.** Critical thinking is impersonal in the sense that mathematics is impersonal. The truth of the sentence "2 + 2 = 4" is not a function of some particular person's moods, values, religion, gender, ethnicity, or such. The logical correctness (validity) of this pattern of reasoning is similarly impersonal:

> If A is greater than B, and
> If B is greater than C, and
> If C is greater than D, *then*
>   A is greater than D

- **Critical thinking offers sustained argumentation (verifiable, rational evidence) for claims supported by logical reasoning, expert testimony, language analysis, and appropriate personal and professional experience.** Good critical thinking offers reasons that will allow any interested, reasonable person to follow the evidence step by step to a rationally sustainable conclusion. Critical thinkers explain why a position is worth holding or why it should be rejected in a way that allows others to follow their reasoning process. Critical thinking skills are the foundation of more specialized forms of logical analysis, scientific, and technical thinking; they are among our best defenses against "self-imposed tutelage."

- **Critical thinking involves rational discourse, the use of reason to order, clarify, identify, and articulate our basic views of reality and truth according to agreed upon standards of evidence.** The ancient Greek philosopher **Socrates (c. 470–399 BCE)** gave his name to one famous form of rational discourse known as the *Socratic method*. The Socratic method is a question-and-answer technique in which the teacher uses guided, sometimes pointed, questions that require the pupil to reason out appropriate answers. Many philosophy professors (and most law schools) use the Socratic method of teaching to foster critical thinking abilities in their students because the Socratic method demands more than just the retention and regurgitation of information. It requires the critical analysis of opinions by carefully defining key terms, drawing inferences, identifying key principles, patterns, and connections, and so forth. Socrates thought that the pursuit of truth should be public and social so that each participant could function as a monitor for other participants. In that way, our individual blind spots could be recognized and filled in by others. One of the most optimistic and charming aspects of Socrates was his insistence that no matter what conclusion was reached by this process (and often the conclusion was that so far nobody is completely correct), every participant and attentive observer benefits—especially those whose errors are identified.

■ **Critical thinkers work at following the evidence wherever it leads in an orderly manner.** One of the signs of good critical thinking is a willingness to accept the best evidence, even when it requires modifying or rejecting a cherished belief or highly desired conclusion. This attitude and the skills that go with it are vital to our culture. Here's an important example of the social significance of good critical skills. Legal experts are disturbed by what one of them characterized as a "growing, serious lack of rationality" among jurors in all parts of the country. Judges, law professors, prosecutors, and defense attorneys note that increasingly jurors are willing to disregard evidence and legally binding instructions, choosing instead to base their verdicts on their feelings, instincts, and uninformed prejudices. The issue here is not just whether a particular jury's verdict is "correct," but the fact that so many legal experts, with so many different perspectives, agree that jurors are increasingly unresponsive to clearly articulated reasons and expert testimony. In legal terms, uncritical juries do not deliberate. Deliberation requires the rational, critical assessment of evidence through forthright discussion and civil argumentation.

■ **Critical thinking alerts us to what is sometimes referred to as the public dimension of argument.** This means that the reasoning used to arrive at conclusions is not mysterious or secret; it is subject to public scrutiny or *public verification* in much the same way that scientific experiments are presented in a way that enables other scientists to verify them. Thus, rational discourse is public discourse, and critical thinking has social and civic aspects, as well as logical and rational ones.

> Socrates thought that the wisest among us are grateful to anyone who helps us identify false beliefs and bad thinking and that getting closer to the truth matters more than protecting our images or "egos" or defending some long-cherished belief. From his perspective, critical thinking is always a social good, and all true patriots participate in it because a healthy democracy depends on enlightened citizens.

WHAT IS *UNCRITICAL* THINKING?

Uncritical thinkers make serious decisions without taking the time, or exerting the effort, to evaluate all sides of an issue critically. Following are some common characteristics of uncritical thinking. As you peruse this list, see if it reminds you of anyone you know. See, too, if some of it doesn't (sadly) remind you of too many television and radio talk shows, web logs, and (perhaps) campus discussions.

■ **Uncritical thinking is characterized by lack of precision and lack of coherence.** Arguments always exhibit poor critical thinking skills when they rely on vague claims to sustain their conclusions. To be effective, avoid using vague, pontificating, or pretentious language.

■ **Uncritical thinking substitutes strong feelings for clearly stated evidence.** Whether you're a television fan or not, you've probably seen enough talk shows to recognize how commonly volume and aggressiveness substitute for rational discourse. Hosts, guests, and invited "experts" shout each other down, all talk at once, sneer, point, gesture wildly—none of which have any bearing on the quality of their evidence or the truth of the points they're trying to make. Even if these methods "work" in the sense of persuading lots of people, they do not get us closer to the truth. As if that were not bad enough, these common substitutes for civilized rational discourse breed cynicism and hostility.

- **Uncritical thinking is often defensive, treating questions and counterarguments as personal insults.** Even though it is sometimes difficult to accept even legitimate criticism, critical thinkers resist defending their "egos" and saving face by going on the attack. Uncritical thinkers, in contrast, zero in on their critics' personal faults, ulterior motives, or alleged ill will. Your position is never strengthened by pointing out other people's flaws or by questioning their motives. Watch out for this one; it is far too common.

- **Uncritical thinking confuses winning and popularity with being right.** Because we are such a results-oriented society, it's tempting to focus too much on "Does it work?" When we do that, we're tempted to admire the sleazy trick that sways the jury—and overlook the fact that our legal system suffers if we treat it like an elaborate game. Your philosophy professor is unlikely to be impressed by such shenanigans. He or she has devoted years to the study of careful reasoning, logic, critical thinking, and methods of persuasion. What seems pretty clever in a presidential debate, on a website, in a courtroom, or on television and radio talk shows won't work at all in a good philosophy class.

- **Uncritical thinking is often impulsive, based on instantaneous judgments strongly influenced by personality, ethnicity, gender, religion, political affiliation, or deeply felt psychological needs.** We've all seen other people succumb to this. Sometimes, you can almost see a blank expression come over others' faces, indicating that nothing anyone says or does will get them to reconsider their position. When people are in this state, they are not reasonable. That is, reasons have no effect on their point of view.

- **Uncritical thinking confuses willed ignorance with knowledgeable confidence.** Willed ignorance is an attitude of indifference to the possibility of either error or enlightenment. Willed ignorance holds onto beliefs regardless of the facts. You can recognize willed ignorance by expressions such as: "I don't care what anybody says, I know X." "Nothing anybody says will ever change my mind about X." "You might be right, but I don't care. I'm going to believe X." People in the throes of willed ignorance refuse to read the literature of their opponents: "No, I've never taken any courses in evolution, I don't have to. I just know those scientists are wrong." "I've never listened to Rush Limbaugh, because he's a bigot." In a nutshell, willed ignorance is unresponsive to reasons, facts, and evidence that challenge preferred points of view.

> Simply put, uncritical thinking accepts or rejects claims according to momentary impulses, unquestioned loyalties, and unreflective personal bias.

WHAT DOES CRITICAL THINKING REQUIRE?

■ **Critical thinking requires the application of appropriate standards of evidence.** What counts as adequate evidence in an informal conversation will probably not be adequate for a philosophy class discussion. Similarly, what's adequate for a class discussion will not be adequate for an essay or term paper.

■ **Critical thinking requires intellectual maturity.** Good critical thinkers do not allow their feelings and personal preferences to control their judgment. When criticized, critical thinkers always ask: Is this criticism valid? If it is, critical thinkers modify their original positions, since their ultimate goal is truth, not saving face.

■ **Critical thinking takes work.** Important issues require careful study. You cannot make reasonable decisions if you do not study issues for yourself—all you can do is react based on partial, second-hand opinions and untested beliefs and prejudices.

■ **Critical thinking requires practice.** Athletes and artists have to work regularly to maintain a certain level of proficiency. Critical thinking skills also require regular "thinking workouts."

■ **Critical thinking requires courage.** It can be difficult to ask: "How do you know that?" People sometimes resent being asked to prove their claims. They may be insulted when we don't merely accept what they say simply because they're our friends or relatives. People may be defensive if our questions reveal that they haven't provided good reasons for their assertions. (Sometimes people don't have any reasons for their assertions.)

■ **Critical thinking requires tact.** Because we depend on one another in our search for truth, it's always best to avoid asking questions in a way that's likely to turn discussions into personal disputes. Angry exchanges reduce, rather than enlarge, our fund of information. The most effective critical thinkers do not shy away from asking necessary questions or pointing out important errors, but they do so with respect and courtesy, fully aware that they might be wrong themselves. As a very general rule, people tend to respond better to clearheaded, focused assertiveness than to self-righteous aggression or unshakable willed ignorance.

CRITICAL THINKING PRACTICES THAT PAY OFF IN THE CLASSROOM—AND BEYOND

- **Distinguish what is important from what is not according to regularly reevaluated principles.** Just as it is unwise to treat important issues as matters of mere preference, it is unwise to subject all issues to a single, excessively detailed analysis. Hairsplitting is the name some philosophers give to the error of applying uncritically excessive scrutiny to minor points. By distinguishing what is important from what is not, good critical thinkers don't get bogged down in a quagmire of tedious minutiae.

- **Pay careful attention to the meanings of terms.** Philosophy is a language-intensive subject. Complex ideas and complex arguments are basic to most philosophical (and all sophisticated) writing. Philosophy, like most academic subjects, has its own technical vocabulary. Many of these technical terms are based on non-English roots. Here are some examples of technical philosophical language: dialectic, noumena, phenomena, eudaimonia, entelechy, a priori, a posteriori, mystification, contradiction, ontological, valid, circular, tautology. You are not unintelligent if you do not know what they mean; you're merely ignorant in the sense of lacking experience and knowledge of these particular terms. You certainly wouldn't try to take a French test without learning some French. If you don't speak French, there is one sense in which you "don't know" what it means to say, "La plume de ma tante est sur la table." Once you make the translation to "My aunt's pen is on the table," everything clears up. The concept is readily comprehended once the language is understood.

- **Be sure you understand exactly what is being said before you do anything else.** One of the most common mistakes beginning philosophy students make is trying to evaluate a claim without first understanding exactly what is being said. For instance, a student once came to my office and said, "I'm having trouble understanding what Aristotle means by *eudaimonia.*" "All right," I said, "why don't you just tell me what the word eudaimonia means." "That's the problem!" he exclaimed. "I can't understand what Aristotle means." "How could you," I asked, "if you have no idea whatsoever what the word itself means?" I sent the student away with specific pages to read in our textbook, pages that had been assigned over a week earlier and which included a definition and explanation of eudaimonia—which, incidentally, is a term Aristotle used to refer to fully realized existence, a state of being fully aware, vital, and alert. It is often translated as "happiness," but happiness is probably too restrictive for the fullness Aristotle had in mind. If my student had said, "I'm not sure what it means to be fully realized," I would have helped him. But he had not done his homework, literally and figuratively. The bottom line is that critical thinking is always about something: terms, facts, causal claims, value judgments. There is no shortcut through memorizing and understanding. Oh yes, after reading the material with attentiveness and care, my student had no trouble understanding eudaimonia well enough to write a clear essay commenting on Aristotle's conception of happiness. He had confused being poorly prepared and uninformed with an inability to understand.

Although it can be frustrating to "just memorize" definitions and details, it's actually a good idea to force yourself to memorize the meanings of new terms—whether you completely understand them or not. Failure to attend to this basic task can create confusion about being confused. I've lost count of the times students have told me that they do not understand what a concept means only to discover that they have failed to familiarize themselves with the essential vocabulary of the day's lesson.

■ **Rely on relevant expertise when appropriate.** No one can possess significant knowledge of all of the kinds of issues that confront people. Socrates insisted that the search for truth cannot begin until we honestly acknowledge the limits of our own knowledge. You can maximize your critical thinking efforts by taking advantage of the accumulated knowledge of experts—just be sure that any experts you consult possess expertise in the field in question, and that most other qualified experts agree with them. Even if you do not know the particulars of a given subject area, you can still apply careful thought to selecting the experts you rely on.

■ **Question any claim that is fundamentally inconsistent with your own carefully evaluated experience (including claims from experts—including me).** I keep a file of deceptive and bogus advertisements. One of my favorites is a flyer for a book of "exam secrets" that guarantees a "great grade point average (GPA)" with no effort. I don't know about your experience, but I've never seen anything capable of guaranteeing a great GPA. Don't you think that such a "secret" would sweep across the nation—no, sweep across the world? The same goes for hair restorers, pills that melt away ugly fat while you sleep (Don't take too many!), 200-miles-per-gallon gadgets to add to your car, and $50.00 Rolex watches for sale on eBay.

■ **Analyze the motives of all interested parties (including your own), without reducing critical scrutiny to character analysis.** Contrary to common opinion, a person's intentions or motives do not tell us much about the reliability of their claims and arguments. When you uncover hidden biases or ulterior motives, you have an additional reason to scrutinize a claimant's assertions. But in the final analysis, it is the asserted evidence that needs to be evaluated, not the arguer.

■ **Distinguish between the arguer and the argument.** A variety of logical fallacies stem from confusing arguers with their arguments. Perhaps the best known is the *argumentum ad hominem*, literally "argument against the man," but now more commonly known as the *personal attack*. The most blatant form of personal attack is the *character assassination*: "You should reject the President's balanced budget proposal because he has been unfaithful to his wife." A more subtle— and therefore more dangerous—version of the personal attack is the *circumstantial personal attack*: "We can ignore Professor Wadsworth's argument supporting a woman's right to abortion on demand. The professor's husband owns an abortion clinic." The *tu quoque* or "look who's talking" is another common form of confusing the arguer with the argument: "You're a fine one to tell me to quit smoking. You could stand to lose a few pounds." Notice that in each of these examples, the character and motives of the arguers do not—of themselves— have any bearing on whether or not the positions being advocated are sound. The President may have unacceptable personal behavior and at the same time advocate a wise budget. Professor Wadsworth's argument may be solid, even if the motive for making it is blind loyalty to her husband. Whether or not my friend is overweight, I should rationally consider his argument against smoking.

■ **Respect differing points of view when they are reasonably defended.** A big problem with contempt for views with which we disagree is that we close ourselves off from the opportunity to learn and grow. (I would certainly hate to think that I will not change any of my fundamental beliefs one tiny bit for the rest of my life.)

■ **Encourage rational discourse by allowing those with whom you disagree to present their point of view for themselves.** This means not interrupting those whose views you abhor by shouting them down before they've finished making their point. Being "correct" is not always enough, if in the process of expressing your views you generate hostility to rational discourse by substituting verbal abuse or physical posturing for a cogent presentation of your views. Everybody loses when issues are "decided" by coercion or the loudest voice.

■ **Welcome legitimate criticism by remaining open to the possibility of error.** If truth is what you seek, then you need to understand the weaknesses in your ideas in order to know whether to improve them or set them aside as unsalvageable. "Playing ostrich" by attempting to avoid criticism does nothing to strengthen a position. A person with cancer has cancer whether or not a doctor diagnoses cancer. Remaining in "denial" may prevent curing a curable condition. Refusing to consider clear, fair criticism does nothing to strengthen your own case and may harm your sense of self-respect. A confident truth seeker has no reason to fear criticism. A lazy or fearful thinker will, however, resist anything that requires a serious reassessment of a cherished belief.

■ **Ask important and relevant questions tactfully and at appropriate times—and wait for a complete answer.** Asking questions serves a twofold purpose: (1) The question-and-answer process can refine and clarify a position. (2) Asking questions and listening to answers keeps the questioner alert and mentally active.

■ **Suspend judgment until both sides of an issue have been given a fair hearing.** This requires being genuinely open to all reasonable, relevant evidence and commits us to more than just token listening designed to create an impression of fairness. If I've already decided before you present your case, then even though I appear to be listening, I'm not really hearing you. Here's one more reason to practice the principle of charity: It opens us up to a wider range of resources and improves our chances of making wise decisions.

■ **Regularly remind yourself that those you disagree with believe that they are being reasonable.** Socrates thought that all evil results from ignorance. He argued that no one willingly chooses evil.

I'm not sure that's always correct, but I do think that most people want to be reasonable, that is, want to have good reasons. At any rate, it's probably best for us to act as if others want to be rational. This humanizes our ideological opponents and reminds us that most of us are fellow travelers in the search for wisdom, truth, and happiness. More often than not, respect for others reduces stress in our own lives. Note, however, that respect for others as serious truth seekers is not the same thing as naïve or gullible acceptance of every idea as plausible. Nor is respecting others an excuse not to keep looking for more truth ourselves.

■ **Research vital issues for yourself.** Avoid relying on the mass media or authority figures for information or viewpoints. For the most part, the mass media are not reliable sources of important factual or technical information. If you want information about health care, vitamins, abortion ethics, race relations, educational patterns, and so forth, you will need to consult textbooks, professional journals, and various experts. Sales brochures put out by health food companies make claims that need to be verified against independent sources. Statistics cited by "pro-life" and "pro-choice" advocates need to be checked—and so on and on. To repeat, critical thinking is an activity, it takes work.

■ **Make a sustained effort to get information from a variety of reliable sources.** I am reminded of a fascinating student I once had in a philosophy class, a very intelligent man in his mid-50s. He was absolutely convinced that the Holocaust of World War II was a big hoax. Nothing I, nor any of his other professors, said or showed him changed his mind. He fell back on his very considerable and expensive library of history books, all supporting his odd contention. This man worked hard to sustain his belief. He read literally hundreds of books—very carefully. When I pointed out that most of these books were published by just a few companies, three of which had the same address, he just shrugged. The moral of the story is that no quantity of biased or weak evidence somehow becomes good evidence.

■ **Take advantage of the Internet and online sources, but don't be seduced by them.** It has been said that the medium is the message and that certainly seems to be the case for many of us when it comes to the Internet. We are impressed by the slick graphics, ease of access and use, instantaneous answers. But the Internet is so vast that it is difficult to know which online sources are reputable, particularly in the case of blogs and Wikipedia, which is part of the "wiki" community that allows anyone to edit, correct, and modify online articles.

7

Critical Writing

Once, when Ernest Hemingway's son Patrick asked his father
to edit a story Patrick had written, Hemingway carefully went
through the manuscript, and returned it to his son. "But,
Papa," Patrick complained, "you've only changed one word."
"If it's the right word, that's a lot," said Hemingway.
A. E. HOTCHNER

Most philosophy courses involve critical writing assignments of
varying complexity and scope. They might include brief essay-
type test questions, out-of-class essays, and longer term paper assignments. The primary goals of critical writing are argumentation,
analysis, and evaluation. Critical writing justifies a conclusion or
interpretation by providing reasonable, relevant, and sufficient evidence to support it. The nature of the evidence depends on the specific way you choose to make your case, and can include any
combination of documented appeals to authoritative sources, language analysis, comparison and contrast, logical argumentation, and
appeals to experience.

Creative writing, by contrast, values novelty, personal expression,
imagination, and emotional impact, among other things. Expository
writing focuses on presenting information in an organized, useful
manner. Creative, expository, and critical writing often occur in the
same text.

THREE CRITICAL STANDARDS
OF EVIDENCE

■ **Relevance.** Evidence offered to support a claim must be directly related to establishing the truth of that claim. Here are two examples of **irrelevant evidence:**

1. Buying a product just because it is a best seller. The fact that millions of people buy X has no direct bearing on whether or not *you* should buy X or whether X is a good product.

2. Rejecting or accepting a claim because you don't like the person making it. The sanitary habits, moral character, religious beliefs, ethnicity, age, gender, and social status of a person are not reasons for you to reject or accept his or her fact claims and arguments.

■ **Reasonableness.** Evidence offered to support a claim must be of such a nature that a disinterested rational person with relevant knowledge and expertise would accept it. Here are two examples of **unreasonable claims:**

1. Claiming that the earth is flat. In order to sustain such a belief, you must somehow discount the consensus among qualified scientific experts that the earth is not flat. This can only be done by assuming that the vast majority of these experts are wrong or that they are involved in a conspiracy. Both assumptions are unreasonable.

2. Claiming that the "medical establishment" can cure cancer but won't because doctors, hospitals, and drug companies make so much money treating it. This claim is an example of the kind of conspiracy theory that flies in the face of experience. It requires that we believe that doctors and scientists would hide the discovery of a cure for cancer rather than publish it and win worldwide acclaim, an almost guaranteed Nobel prize, tons of money for research grants, and a place in medical history. Further, such theories require the unreasonable assumption that countless other people can or will keep such an important secret for years. Lastly, the claim unfairly characterizes most members of the medical establishment as greedy, money-hungry opportunists.

■ **Sufficiency.** There must be enough reasonable, relevant evidence to support the claim. Here are two examples of **insufficient evidence:**

1. Drawing conclusions about members of other ethnic groups based only on your own experiences with them or what you

observe in the mass media. Even the most sociable and sophisticated among us do not have enough personal experience to draw conclusions about entire ethnic groups. The mass media present images carefully selected and edited for dramatic or novelty appeal. The mass media cannot be relied on to provide a thorough, representative view of life.

2. Deciding that philosophy is boring based on your experiences with one course or one book. One course from one instructor is simply not sufficient to draw conclusions about a subject.

■ **An example of a claim that is both unreasonable and insufficient.** The student described earlier who denied the existence of the Holocaust based on his extensive reading of hundreds of volumes of biased literature. By only consulting books from a few publishers with an ax to grind, this man, in effect, limited the scope of his support. A million dollars in play money is not sufficient to buy one dollar's worth of apples.

BASIC FEATURES OF GOOD CRITICAL WRITING

Here are some of the most common features of good critical writing, regardless of length:

■ **Good critical writing treats its readers as reasonable persons who care about truth.** Even the finest critical writers are "wrong" occasionally, but wrong in thoughtful, worthwhile ways.

■ **Good critical writing clearly identifies its main point (thesis) early.** Your reader should not have to read three or four pages, or even three or four paragraphs, to figure out what your main point is (or worse yet, have to guess). Your thesis (main point) should be made clear in the opening paragraph.

■ **Good critical writing avoids evasive weasel claims.** The primary function of a weasel claim is to leave its author a way around criticism. Weasel claims make and evade a point at the same time. Consider this example: "It seems to me that Plato might have meant Z." Take a stand. Think. Did Plato mean Z or not?

■ **Good critical writing documents its case so that readers can verify all important factual and scholarly claims for themselves.** Common forms of documentation include footnotes or endnotes.

77

■ **Good critical writing avoids vague attributions.** *Vague attributions,* as the term implies, cite general sources without providing the details needed to establish their reasonableness, relevance, or sufficiency: "Virtually all Christians oppose abortions." "Most feminist philosophers favor abortion on demand." Use of vague attributions is almost always an indication of inferior research. Vague attributions never provide support for an argument because they don't tell the reader enough. Precisely, which Christians or feminists hold these views, if any? Are they important Christians or feminists, or members of fringe groups? Further, by not clearly identifying their sources, vague attributions don't tell us how current their content is. To the discerning reader, vague attributions suggest sloppy, uncritical reasoning.

> Vague attributions often signal bias and propaganda: Republican party candidates vaguely refer to "the Democrats" and Democratic party candidates vaguely refer to "the Republicans." Various activist groups attribute offensive beliefs to "atheists," "secular humanists," "liberals," "fundamentalists," "white people," and "minorities." Without specifying precisely who said exactly what, and in what context, claims supported by vague attributions function as propaganda, not evidence. Avoid sweeping, vague attributions. They never strengthen your case, and almost always weaken it.

■ **Good critical writing avoids unsubstantiated appeals to "common sense" or "common knowledge."** "Everybody knows. . ." "Decent people agree. . ." Such sweeping generalizations suffer from the same weaknesses as vague attributions. Further, they are unhelpful, if not meaningless, since they are either obviously false (as in the first example), or contain loaded, unclear terms that substitute for evidence ("decent" in the second example).

■ **Good critical writing is organized.** It contains an opening statement of the thesis or topic, a main body, and a clearly identified summation–conclusion. Every paragraph is relevant. The text moves toward a clearly defined goal.

FIVE GREAT WRITING TIPS

■ **GREAT WRITING TIP NUMBER 1:** Start writing right away, and plan on revising your finished paper at least once.

■ **GREAT WRITING TIP NUMBER 2:** *Look at* your finished paper. Are the paragraphs one sentence long? Or one page long?

If the paragraphs are uniformly long or short, the work may be poorly organized.

■ **GREAT WRITING TIP NUMBER 3: Write the final version of the introduction and conclusion last.** Always match your introduction to your conclusion. A simple way to do this is to write only a tentative introduction to use as you develop your essay or paper. When you're finished with the body of the paper, word your conclusion in terms of what you've actually shown—and then write your final version of the introduction.

If you've shown A, B, C, and D, your conclusion might include something like: "In this essay I began by showing A. Having done that, I explained how B and C follow from A. This led to my main point, D."

After you've written the conclusion, write the final version of your introduction using key words and phrases from the conclusion. For example: "In this essay I begin by showing A. I next explain how B and C follow from A. This leads directly to my main point, D."

Framing your essay with a matching introduction and conclusion that accurately describe its content does three vital things: (1) It tells the reader what to expect. (2) It does what it promised to do. (3) It reminds the reader that it has done what it promised to do. Using key words and phrases in all three parts of the essay gives your work a polished coherence.

One of the most embarrassing, avoidable errors inattentive writers make is not matching the introduction and conclusion with each other and with the body of the paper. If you begin with the announcement that you will show A, B, C, and D, and only show A, B, and C, you will have failed to substantiate your thesis. This is true even if D is a minor point.

Always double check the introduction and conclusion after you've finished the final version of the body of the paper. **CAUTION: This tip is not a substitute for good content. It will not obscure a weak effort.**

■ **GREAT WRITING TIP NUMBER 4: Let your paper get "cold" before you make your last editing pass.** Set your paper aside long enough to develop some critical distance before you make your last revision. You will spot major and minor problems much easier if you can read your own work with a fresh eye—and a sufficient lapse of time is the best way to do this.

■ **GREAT WRITING TIP NUMBER 5: Form always matters, but it's not all that matters.** College professors complain of a tendency for many students to put more care into producing slick-looking papers—fancy titles, neat graphics, elegant paper, etc.—than into producing substantive content. No doubt today's personal computers, high-quality printers, and powerful word processors make this tempting. Try to resist. And if you can't resist, at least make sure your paper's content has priority.

HOW TO PICK A TOPIC

■ **Start thinking about possible topics as soon as the assignment is made.** Flag passages in the text that might make good topics—even if you're not personally interested in them. At this stage, you want as many ideas as possible. Ideas breed ideas. Jot down inconsistencies, annoyances, or questions, anything that provoke a response from you. Don't trust yourself to remember potential topics—write them down.

■ **Think small.** One of the most common errors introductory philosophy students make in choosing a paper or essay topic is underestimating the amount of clarification and argumentation most critical writing requires. As a result, students sometimes pick huge topics that require writing a whole book.

> If you don't have much experience writing critically, follow this rule of thumb: If you think a topic is too small, it's probably about right. It's better to have "too much" evidence than not enough.

■ **Word your topic precisely.** Vague topics tend to result in vague papers. Note the difference between these topics: "Existentialism" and "Nietzsche's Claim That God Is Dead Cannot Be True." The second topic refers to a specific concept discussed in a textbook. The narrowness of the second topic is a virtue. It helps define and limit the writer's task. A general topic does not reflect an idea; it only indicates an area.

■ **Don't take your topic personally.** You don't need to care about a subject to write well about it. Pick a topic that you can write well about in the amount of time you have. Be practical in your selection, considering what's going on in other courses you're taking, your job and family obligations, and your own actual work habits and abilities.

■ **Forget about inspiration.** Don't fall into the trap of waiting for inspiration. Pick a topic as soon as you know the nature of the assignment. Waiting for inspiration may be a form of procrastination. Besides, inspiration may not come.

■ **Unless you are an excellent critical writer, avoid defending your most deeply held personal beliefs.** For whatever reason, most of us are better at spotting weaknesses in ideas we dislike than we are at rationally supporting our own beliefs. A graded assignment in a philosophy class may not be the place to find out if you are an exception. Some of the poorest papers philosophy professors receive are written in defense of the writer's most cherished beliefs. Their chief deficiency is the substitution of heartfelt conviction and personal testimony for cogent argument and balanced documentation.

Remember: There is no perfect topic. Don't make more out of your topic selection than you have to. Your paper is not your last and only chance to say something on this subject. Your topic needs to be relevant to the course, adequate in scope yet not overwhelming, and researchable, given your current resources. That's all.

A QUICK GUIDE TO GETTING BETTER GRADES ON WRITING ASSIGNMENTS

■ **Pick a topic early and don't change it (unless absolutely necessary).** Use the guidelines above to pick your topic. Then get right into it. Do any necessary research early. This will maximize the amount of time you have to process and refine your ideas.

■ **Is instructor approval necessary? If so—obtain it.** You'd be surprised how many students overlook or deliberately omit this step. Always a dangerous decision.

■ **Just write.** As soon as you have finished your initial preparation (which may range from studying a portion of your textbook to more substantial independent research), write something. Write quickly, ignoring organization, grammar, and spelling—for the moment.

See where your mind wants to go. The act of writing usually enhances the critical thinking process.

Beware of procrastinating. It's easy to joke about procrastinating about term papers, but a 2002 study by Fuschia M. Sirois and Timothy A. Pychyl of 374 undergraduates linked procrastination to "avoidant coping styles." Avoidant coping styles involve neglecting rather than confronting problems that cause anxiety—like thinking up topics for term papers. According to Sirois and Pychyl, more is at stake here than late papers. Avoidant styles are associated with smoking, heavy drinking, and a reluctance to deal with serious health problems.

- **Form a semi-rough draft.** Once you've written a rough draft, you're ready to give it a more polished form. Shape paragraphs, move ideas around, elaborate, explain, clarify.

- **Define all key terms when you introduce them.** Be sure to specify exactly how you are using any key technical terms. Do not use a conventional dictionary to define technical terms. Conventional dictionaries only provide common, socially correct usage. Doctors and lawyers use medical and legal dictionaries. Use your textbook, primary sources, references like the *Encyclopedia of Philosophy,* and a good philosophy dictionary when you need technical definitions to define key philosophical terms. (See the Beginning Philosopher's Bibliography for examples of good philosophical dictionaries.)

- **After you have written your first complete polished version, put it away and forget about it.** Let your work get cold. You'll need time to do this. That's why you picked a topic quickly and got to work early. Set the paper aside for a day or two at least—a week is better. This will help you acquire the critical distance you'll need to take an objective look at your work.

- **Critically revise.** Once you've established "critical distance" by setting your paper aside for a time, you're ready for careful revising. Read your paper as if you were grading it. Mark it up. As you read, ask yourself: Is the thesis clearly stated? Does each step lead logically to what follows? Are important points supported with clearly stated reasons? Are terms used consistently? Are claims supported with documented sources, as needed? Does the paper make its case? Improve the text as you answer these questions with your thesis clearly in mind.

- **If necessary, modify your original thesis.** Once they have begun work on a topic, it's common for philosophical writers to discover that their original plan can be improved by selective modification. Perhaps too much is included, so some pruning is in order. Or perhaps what originally looked like a minor point has turned out to be crucial, so shifting and beefing up are in order. The point is, writing is not like captaining a ship. You're not honor bound to go down with a leaky vessel. Abandon a shaky topic, if it can't be salvaged. Sometimes, there's no way to know that topic won't work for you until you have a go at it. (Changing topics should be a last resort. That's why picking a topic early is so important.)

■ **Don't be seduced by computerized spell-checkers and grammar-checkers.** Spell-checkers don't always contain technical philosophical terms. Spell-checking cannot catch the misuse of homonyms (words that sound alike) such as "two," "to," and "too." They may not catch correctly spelled but entirely inappropriate words. They don't catch omissions or redundancies. Different grammar-checkers have different protocols. None of them is entirely foolproof. You need to proofread your work even if you use these aides. To see why, study the anonymous poem that pops up on electronic bulletin boards:

> I have a spelling checker,
> It came with my PC;
> It plainly marks four my revue
> Mistakes I cannot sea.
> I've run this pome threw it,
> I'm sure your pleased to no,
> It's letter perfect in its weigh,
> My checker tolled me sew.
> I only rote it one thyme,
> Two let you here it rhyme,
> Bee for I drank sum tee,
> And inn my bed eye clime.

■ **Don't confuse a good-looking, properly spelled, grammatically correct paper with a good paper.** Your professor has a right to expect a neat, grammatically correct paper. That's the minimum in philosophy classes, not the maximum. The mechanics of your paper should be "transparent," unnoticed by the reader. A mechanically correct paper allows its content to shine forth. Your philosophy professor may or may not mark grammatical errors, but he or she will certainly note them—and they will almost certainly damage the critical content of your writing.

■ **Stop when you've made your point.** Don't pad your paper. Few philosophy instructors are impressed by sheer volume. You're probably better off saying less very precisely and coherently, than saying more sloppily. As with all advice, make sure this suggestion applies to your circumstances. If your instructor places a premium on length, then pick your topic accordingly. You're still going to need to be clear and precise, however, no matter how long your paper is. Even if you have to write a long paper—don't pad it.

■ **Follow instructions.** Let's admit it. Many of the requirements instructors insist on are just their preferences. In the great scheme of things, who cares whether you use staples or paper clips, plastic covers or title sheets? The person grading your work cares, that's who. And that's a pretty good reason to follow instructions. It may not matter in the grand scheme of things whether you use footnotes, endnotes, or in-text citations. If, however, your instructor says endnotes, it matters to your grade. Use whatever style guide or manual your instructor requires. If none is specified, ask for guidance. Use the kind of paper, binder, and toner or ink color specified. Follow instructions regarding title pages and paper clips, margins, bibliographies, font size, spacing, and due dates. If your instructor has not specified these things, ASK. Don't assume. Get clear information right away.

■ **Document all sources.** Any time you are using someone else's idea without significant modification, you need to document its originator. You have nothing to lose by citing good sources, and a great deal to lose by plagiarizing them, since penalties range from flunking an assignment to expulsion from college. (See earlier section regarding plagiarism.)

> Ironically, not citing sources almost always results in a poorer grade than crediting sources would have, because citing authorities and experts of established reputation adds their expertise and authority to your own excellent ideas. When you don't give credit to established experts, you deprive your paper of important support.

■ **Use a good general, college-level dictionary and an approved style guide.** Simply assume that spelling and grammar count—don't embarrass yourself by asking if they count. Consult your instructor regarding preferred style guidelines. See the Beginning

Philosopher's Bibliography at the back of this book for the names of some good style guides.

- **Type your work.** Other things being equal, neatly typed assignments get higher grades than handwritten ones. Take advantage of this. (But neat garbage is still garbage, and neatly typed garbage is a waste of everybody's time.)

- **Stick to the length specified.** Unless explicitly told otherwise, use conventional margins, double spacing, and use 10- or 12-point font if you have a word processor. Play fair. Don't try to pad a thin paper with huge printing and exaggerated margins, and don't exceed length requirements with small print, small margins, and space-and-a-half printing. To be safe, try to get a specified word count rather than page length.

- **Proofread your final draft.** It is much better to make one or two neat corrections by hand than to ignore typographical errors, spelling errors, bad grammar, and gross inconsistencies. If you have more than two corrections on a page, redo it. This is another reason to allow plenty of time for the entire writing process, from topic selection to typing or printing the final version.

- **Keep at least one copy of your paper in a safe place.** Your instructor is not the one who will suffer if your paper is lost or damaged.

- **Turn in a high-quality original or photocopy, not a faint, smudged, or black-edged one.**

- **Do not use onionskin, easy-erase, or colored paper.**

- **Plan ahead to get to school early on the due date.** Some instructors penalize late papers. Allow for possible transportation problems and other contingencies.

- **If you need special consideration, talk to your instructor as soon as you are aware of special needs.** Don't be embarrassed to request special consideration, if you really need it. On the other hand, don't think of just being busy or apprehensive about writing a paper as a special need. Most students are very busy and at least moderately nervous about turning in written work.

- **Always study your graded paper.** Try to understand why your instructor gave you that grade. If you need more explanation than is provided with the graded paper, politely request it.

- **Cool off before you decide you were cheated on your grade.** If you feel that your grade is inaccurate, after setting the paper aside for a few days and carefully rereading it, courteously request a rereading by your instructor.

■ **If your instructor does not return graded papers, make an appointment to review and discuss your paper during office hours.** If you plan to discuss your paper with the instructor, be sure to give him or her time to review it before the discussion.

FOUR WRITING SAMPLES
FOR YOU TO GRADE

One of the best ways to improve your critical writing is by reading other people's critical writing. In some writing courses, students exchange essays and rough drafts of papers for the purpose of offering positive criticism. They help one another identify strengths and weaknesses, and get a better idea of how good writing differs from poor writing.

The following short essays were written by students in an introduction to philosophy course. They were written in class as part of an announced closed-book test. Two weeks before the test, the instructor distributed a list of questions from which the actual test question would be selected. The review questions all referred to specific topics covered in Chapter 17 of the textbook *Archetypes of Wisdom: An Introduction to Philosophy,* Sixth Edition. Nietzsche's claim that "God is dead" was discussed at length in class, as well.

As you read each of the unedited essays, use these questions as guidelines for your evaluation. See if you think the essays clearly and directly answer the question: **What did Nietzsche mean by the "death of God"? Why is the issue important? Do you agree with Nietzsche? Explain.**

Here are some questions to ask as you read the students' essays: Would an intelligent reader who is unfamiliar with Nietzsche's idea get a clear introduction to its meaning from the essay? Does the essay give evidence of familiarity with the assigned readings? For instance, does it use specific examples or concepts from the text? Are the sentences grammatically correct and is the essay well organized (given the time constraints of an in-class essay)?

Based on your answers to these questions, what grade would you give each essay? Why? (It's a good idea to read all four responses before assigning grades to any of them.)

SAMPLE ESSAY 1

What did Nietzsche mean by the "death of God"? Why is the issue important? Do you agree with Nietzsche? Explain.

He means that after God created everything, he had used up a lot of his omipotencey and could only do so much. Nietzeshe was strange. Many people did not like him. He did not like them either. Nietzshe may have been a Nazi but its hard to tell. I felt sorry for Nietzshe but think that God is not dead. But I can't prove it. So maybe he is.

SAMPLE ESSAY 2

What did Nietzsche mean by the "death of God"? Why is the issue important? Do you agree with Nietzsche? Explain.

Nietzsche did not think God ever lived, so technically, he (God) is dead. Well, not really dead, but more or less imaginary, like a myth. When he said that God is dead he meant that nobody took God seriously anymore. He was talking about the 1800s. In those days, people believed in factories and the Industrial Revolution more than God. I think Nietzsche had a point. Today we believe in the Internet and medicine more than God. I am not sure if that is good or bad, but it is worth thinking about.

SAMPLE ESSAY 3

What did Nietzsche mean by the "death of God"? Why is the issue important? Do you agree with Nietzsche? Explain.

Nietzsche meant that the thought of God was not a good thought. In other words, God was a bad idea in those days because people didn't think much about God. They thought about other things. Not about God. So was God dead or was he just a bad idea? And did other people think God is a dead idea? Nietzsche had a point. He was a deep thinker.

SAMPLE ESSAY 4

What did Nietzsche mean by the "death of God"? Why is the issue important? Do you agree with Nietzsche? Explain.

"God is dead. We have killed God!" Those are the famous words of Friedrich Nietzsche. The idea of the death of God is stated in "Thus Spoke Zarathustra," a long story Nietzsche wrote about life "after God."

Nietzsche hated Christianity because he thought that Christian ethics treat adults like children and make us weak. Nietzsche wanted us to be strong, to be "supermen" not scared slaves waiting for God's protection.

Nietzsche did not actually believe that God as a person or being dropped dead one day, but that society was growing up and people were taking care of themselves. So we have not killed God in a physical way, but with science. We just don't know it yet, he says, so we still think that God is important to us. But when we see how far we have evolved, we will forget God. That is how God is dead, in Nietzsche's opinion.

Do I agree? Yes and no. I am a Christian, so I do believe in God (as do Jews and Muslims). But I can see how secular our society is. Sometimes I find myself putting my faith in science and technology more than God. So, in a way, God dies for me. But does not believing in something make it dead? I hope not. But I worry about making technology a god. So, I guess I agree with Nietzsche without agreeing that God is dead. Does that make sense?

A CRITICAL LOOK AT THE FOUR
SAMPLE ESSAYS

You're probably wondering what grades the four sample essays got in "real life."

■ **Sample Essay 1 received an F.** Its most glaring error is that it is flat out wrong. It completely misinterprets Nietzsche's notion. The death of God refers to a complex, cultural shift, not the literal death or weakness of a being. Note, too, the inconsistent and incorrect misspellings of "Nietzsche"—unforgivable always, and embarrassing, given that the correct spelling occurs in the question. Nietzsche's unpopularity is never connected to the topic and the Nazi comment confirms the reader's suspicion that this student was inattentive in class and did not study the text. The "conclusion" is just padding—words to no purpose.

■ **Sample Essay 2 received a B.** The first sentence lets the reader know that the author of Sample Essay 2 is familiar with the assignment. The author then proceeds to develop the idea, referring to the cultural and historical critique that frames Nietzsche's notion of the death of God. Nietzsche was indeed concerned with the shift from a

Judeo-Christian ethic to a "higher" ethic of self-reliance. The reference to the Industrial Revolution is good, but not adequately developed. The closing references to today's widespread faith in the Internet and medicine are allusions to in-class discussions and confirm the author's solid grasp of the topic.

- **Sample Essay 3 received a C–.** This essay makes one correct point, albeit poorly, namely that the death of God refers to the death of a way of thinking and repeats that notion in different words, as if repetition is evidence or explanation. Without elaboration and explanation, the promising assertion that ". . . in those days . . . people didn't think much about God. They thought about other things. Not about God." falls flat. It is difficult to tell how well this writer grasps Nietzsche's position. The question "So was God dead or was he just a bad idea?" could be the beginning of a cogent analysis, but, alas, it is not developed. This is a difficult essay to grade. It is "close," "intriguing," and "teasing." There is no way to know if its lack of follow-up and precision are symptoms of a failure to read and study the material or of the sort of haste that sometimes occurs due to exam pressure. Be forewarned: Although some instructors interpret such ambiguities to the writer's advantage, most instructors do not. In the end, this essay is merely "okay."

- **Sample Essay 4 received an A.** This essay contains multiple references to the assigned readings, making it very clear that its author had studied them. Explicit references to Zarathustra, the Nietzschean notions of "supermen" and slaves, science and (implicitly) evolution indicate that this author is familiar with and understands the assigned readings. Topical references to today and to Jews and Muslims are effective, as is the personal acknowledgment of the author's religious orientation, which is done in a judicious way. The closing is compelling and encouraging to the writer's professor. It shows that here is a person who is applying class material to his or her life, who is thinking. An excellent job on a closed-book essay that was part of a larger test.

CHARACTERISTICS OF GOOD AND BAD ESSAYS

Many students think that essay assignments and essay tests are "subjective" in the sense that they have no one "right answer." That's not always true, and even when there is no one "right answer," it is still possible to rank the quality of essays in ways that are not superficially and capriciously arbitrary, as we have just seen. Still, you may have had the common experience of being absolutely convinced that you were cheated on your grade for a writing assignment because you wrote "the same thing" as your friend who got a higher grade. The difficulty in determining that you've been cheated rests on the fact that no matter how similar two essays are, they are not exactly the same—unless at least one of them is plagiarized.

Grades are affected by the order in which topics are covered, word choice, organization (paragraphing), sentence structure, nature and number of examples, degree of specificity, and so forth. Your essay may be very similar to your friend's, but your professor is probably responding to the *whole essay effect,* as well as to individual aspects that your essay may share with your friend's.

Does this mean that essay grades are subjective in the sense of being capricious or arbitrarily relative? In fact, there is a high degree of consistency among grading standards of experienced professors. Professor W may be slightly tougher than Professor Y, so that a B+ from Professor W is roughly equivalent to an A from Professor Y, but the relative rankings of their grades will tend to conform. That means that it is highly unlikely that an essay that gets an A from Professor Y would get a D or an F from Professor W.

In doing the research for this book, I have identified certain common characteristics that affect the way many professors grade essays. Knowing what these are can help you write better essays and papers (since essays and papers share many fundamental features). Here's what I found, which, incidentally, often reflected my own grading practices.

- **Spelling and grammar always matter. Period.** Having a grammatically correct essay is not a substitute for not knowing the material, but poor grammar and spelling detract from even the best ideas.

- **Length matters, but not in a simplistic way.** Essays that call for explanation, elaboration, or critical evaluation must be long enough to cover everything asked for. From that point on, however, length is not a reliable indicator of quality. A lot of irrelevant, unclear, or incorrect material only underscores lack of preparation. Avoid padding your essays.

- **Good essays answer the question as it is asked.** This is just another form of following instructions, which is always fundamental. Writing brilliantly about something else, even something closely related to the assignment, is not a substitute for showing your professor that you understand the specific material he or she wants to test you on.

- **Good essays offer reasonable, relevant, sufficient evidence to support their claims.** Poor essays tend to settle for merely making assertions, or offering vague or sweeping statements as support.

- **Good essays are specific.** Good essays use precise, correct terms and examples from assigned readings. Good essays refer to individuals by name on a regular basis. Poor essays use "he," "she," or "they" too often.

- **Good essays make it very clear that their writers are familiar with both assigned readings and lectures and class discussions.** This is another way of being specific, rather than general and vague.

- **Good essays and papers reflect organized thought.** Good writing is well structured and organized; it reflects careful studying and planning. Jumbled, chaotic take-home writing implies lack of preparation and effort. Jumbled, chaotic in-class writing is more difficult to interpret, but assuming that you have the prerequisite language skills for a philosophy class, your professor will probably interpret poorly organized work as evidence of a lack of preparation—and possibly comprehension.

- **Excellent essays and papers provide unique examples and explanations.** Excellent academic writing reflects a solid grasp of course material, but in its own unique voice. It does not just repeat examples and explanations from the textbook and lectures.

- **Excellent essays and papers draw conclusions and make inferences that go beyond class material.** These can be in the form of questions, criticisms, identification of inconsistencies, and so forth.

- **Six common weaknesses.** Essays and papers decline in quality with each of the following avoidable mistakes:

  - **Misspelled names and key terms.** This implies that you have not read the material at all, or that you have not studied it carefully. At the very least, you should identify all key figures and technical terms and memorize their correct spellings.

  - **Factual errors.** Factual errors include attributing ideas to the wrong source or distorting a philosopher's views.

  - **Irrelevant material.** Weak essays rely on irrelevant personal comments and anecdotes ("I had a lot of trouble picking a topic. At first I was going to write about Plato . . ."), or distracting analyses of concepts that do not directly answer the question as it is framed.

  - **Unexplained or unsupported key assertions.** Sample Essay 3 is a classic example of this error. Repeating the same point in different words is a variant of this mistake since merely repeating something more than once does not somehow become additional evidence for its truth.

■ **Merely listing lots of ideas.** Students who receive lower grades than they were expecting sometimes express considerable frustration when they feel that they have "included everything you said was important." Including all important material is only a necessary step in writing a good analytic or critical essay, however. Because a critical essay is different from a summary or report, a mere "laundry list" approach is not sufficient. A list or summary is never a substitute for a cogent analysis.

■ **Numerous mechanical errors.** At the very least, numerous errors indicate that the writer has not proofread his or her work. More seriously, numerous basic errors of grammar can identify a need for remedial writing courses; this is always a disappointment, but not something the motivated college student can avoid dealing with.

A HANDY CHECKLIST FOR BETTER CRITICAL WRITING

Review this list whenever you write, proofread, or revise.

____ Is the first paragraph so clear that any reader will know exactly what the topic is?

____ Are your topic and conclusion paragraphs consistent?

____ Does the first or second paragraph clearly describe your strategy for dealing with your topic?

____ Does your essay or paper use specific examples and language to show that you are familiar with the assigned readings and any other important material?

____ Does your essay or paper end with a clear and obvious summation and conclusion, keyed precisely and directly to what you say in the body of the text?

____ Does your paper have a complete, properly formatted (and punctuated) list of works cited?

____ Have you followed all formatting instructions discussed in "Appendix A: A Simplified Style Guide For Excellent Papers"— or the guide required by your instructor?

____ Are all sentences grammatically correct?

____ Are all sentences punctuated correctly?

____ Are all technical terms spelled correctly?

____ Is your essay or paper well organized?

____ Are all sources properly documented?

____ Have you proofread the final version of your essay or paper?

A NOTE ABOUT TECHNOLOGY
AND THE INTERNET

Like so many other things, the Internet's strengths are also its weaknesses. These include virtually unlimited freedom of expression, communication, and variety. But unmonitored openness and freedom requires extra caution on our part, particularly when we turn to the Internet for technical information and advice. The ease with which individuals and groups can establish their own websites and "publish" information via web logs (blogs), newsrooms, chat rooms, intranets, and e-mailed newsletters allows just about anyone to claim just about anything—whether or not they know much of anything at all about it.

As a rule, works published in academic, scientific, and technical fields have to pass muster through what's known as "blind peer reviewing." Thus, you can assume that an article published in the *American Philosophical Quarterly* "competed" with other articles for publication, and that each submitted article was evaluated by professional philosophers who specialize in the philosophical issues discussed in the articles. With rare exceptions, this process assures that important professional standards have been met and that the authors of the published articles know whereof they write. In the sciences, peer review and publication of experimental protocols and data reinforce basic principles of scientific method: Verification or rejection by disinterested—even hostile—peers.

This time-consuming process isn't perfect, of course, and it does not guarantee that academic and professional publications are right in any simple sense. Nonetheless, the process matters, and it matters a great deal, because it imposes agreed-upon standards of expression and evidence on authors and researchers; it matters because it subjects our work to public peer scrutiny. Private, personally controlled publications, such as blogs and websites of unknown origin, are not entitled to a presumption of objectivity.

The exponential proliferation of websites available from unknown and unvetted sources means that scholars using the Internet need to exercise hypercritical judgment as they "surf the Net." There is nothing magical about the Internet that makes information gleaned there automatically worthwhile or reliable. And it's pretty easy to set up good-looking websites with great graphics and lots of links to other websites—often of equally mysterious origin or quality.

Lastly, a website's ranking on Google, Yahoo!, or other search sites is not a function of its veracity or the quality of its content. It's only another measure of popularity.

■ **Treat online resources as you would any other sources.** Be especially cautious when relying on fact claims and assertions from untested, unknown, or unidentifiable sources, just as you would if confronted with hardcopy sources of unknown pedigree. (And, of course, you should always critically assess claims made by even the most prestigious of sources—whether hardcopy, digital, or online.)

> It's become deceptively simple: You can have a search box, type in a phrase or a few words, and immediately receive hundreds or thousands of articles. . . . A lot of this full text that is being put into the database is of questionable quality. At least back in the days of paper resources, you had indexes that were indexing a few hundred journals. Now you multiply that by hundreds, and lot of the publications are not that high-quality. . . . It's now much easier to get into a whole lot of trouble so much faster.—Steven J. Bell, library director at Philadelphia University.

■ **Resist using the Internet as your sole source of information.** It is one thing to use the Internet as one source among others, and quite another to use the Internet exclusively because it is easier to download whatever you find than it is to do more substantial research that includes hardcopy sources. You'll deprive yourself if you ignore the Internet and you'll deprive yourself if you ignore hardcopy sources, as well.

- **More information is not always better.** Search engines operate on different protocols. For example, Google, the most-used Internet search engine, ranks pages according to how often they're linked and cited by other pages. Other search engines grant pride of place to websites that pay for higher rankings. Some specialized databases lump hundreds or thousands of sources of mixed quality together. Often, the best information has to be hunted for. It may be the 5th, 105th, or 10,005th page returned by a search engine.

- **Do not confuse the mode of delivery with what is delivered.** It is tempting to equate form with substance. That's why we tend to give more credence to impressive-looking books than to poorly produced ones. Some people even assume that if something is published in a magazine or newspaper or on a fancy website, it must be reliable. This tendency to confuse the method of delivery with what is delivered carries over to CD-ROMs and computer-generated projects printed on high-quality paper. Impressive graphics, web animation, drop-down lists of hyperlinks, and sound can greatly enhance the content of online and digital sources. But the very success of computer-assisted communications entices entrepreneurs to come up with increasingly attractive—and often genuinely useful—offerings. Keep in mind, however, that in spite of all the hype, a CD-ROM or online encyclopedia, for example, is still an encyclopedia. If an encyclopedia is an appropriate source of information, and a good CD-ROM or online version offers the benefits of easy search features and fast copying, then by all means take advantage of it. But if you wouldn't use a standard encyclopedia, don't settle for a high-tech one just because it's easy and convenient to do so. Similarly, if a print magazine or pamphlet isn't an adequate source for your project, neither is a high-tech one, no matter how many "hits" its website generates or how high it's ranked by a search engine or online database.

- **Technology will fail—count on it.** Although there are legitimate technological excuses for failing to meet assignment deadlines and paper due dates, they are surprisingly rare. Printer jams, just like traffic jams, bathroom jams, dead car batteries, and alarm clocks that don't alarm are all the regular stuff of everyday life. As such, they are *generally foreseeable,* especially disk crashes, Zip disks that lose their zip, power outages, Internet freezes, website glitches, and more. That means that you should anticipate problems and guard against them in budgeting time to complete your research and to prepare and deliver the final draft of your paper.

■ **The more prep time you have, the fewer good excuses there are for not being prepared.** This is especially so in the case of major assignments for which you have been given substantial lead time. If, for instance, you have been given four weeks to research and write a paper, your professor may be underwhelmed upon learning that you were still working on it at 3 a.m. the morning it was due, or that you arrived at the college computer center to begin typing it one day before it was due and discovered that a virus had shut down the college's computers.

■ **Don't be afraid to request special consideration when you have genuinely extenuating technological circumstances that are beyond your control.** But don't violate your own sense of self-respect by pleading special circumstances when the circumstances are not special.

■ **Back up, back up, back up, and save, save, save.** Personally, I think there ought to be a law against accepting any late work from students who haven't backed up and saved their work all along. Fortunately, I'm not in control of things. Nobody is—and that's why you and I should always back up, back up, back up, and save, save, save.

A NOTE ABOUT
"DISTANCE EDUCATION"

Distance education (DE) refers to courses taken away from the main campus. DE includes televised courses, courses on audiotape, and, increasingly, online courses offered over the Internet.

■ **On the plus side.** The obvious advantages of DE courses are convenience (many of them allow you to work at your own pace in a location of your own choosing), flexibility (many DE offerings are provided around the clock, freeing you from the confines of rigidly scheduled semesters or quarters), and accessibility (no matter where you live, you can sign up for courses at colleges around the world). An added bonus in some DE programs is the opportunity to "design your own degree." You decide which courses you want to take and the college customizes your degree requirements.

- **On the negative side (maybe).** DE courses are great for certain students, but they are a disaster for anyone who has trouble keeping commitments, sticking to a schedule, and keeping track of details. It is not surprising that drop rates for DE courses are higher than those for traditional-style courses. This doesn't mean that one kind of course is better than another, but it does reflect an easily overlooked risk with DE courses. With increased flexibility comes increased responsibility. If you elect to try DE, consider starting with one or two courses to see if you like being on your own.

- **DE civility.** If you take online courses, remember that you are a member of an extended cyber community. If you are expected to post or read e-essays, do so in a timely fashion. Just as you wouldn't hog class time in a physically present class setting, don't hog cyber discussions. Just as you wouldn't drop by your instructor's office whenever you felt like, don't fire off e-mail after e-mail. You get the picture?

> Information is readily available to us: where shall wisdom be found?
> —Harold Bloom

Conclusion

How long do you put off thinking yourself worthy
of the best things . . . what sort of teacher are you still
waiting for, that you put off improving yourself
until he comes? You are not a [child] anymore,
but already . . . full grown.
EPICTETUS

If you've learned anything from this book, I hope it's that you have a great deal of influence over your grade in philosophy and over your entire college experience. The tips and advice in *How to Get the Most Out of Philosophy* can help you avoid certain pitfalls and increase your chances of success—but they cannot provide you with the will and drive necessary to succeed.

The wish to do well is common. The will and sustained drive to do what's necessary to do well are less common. Regardless of your past performance in school and regardless of your "native ability," you can take deliberate, time-tested steps to improve your chances of learning philosophy and getting a good grade in the process. There are no substitutes for regular, organized work, however.

You probably won't be able (or want) to follow every suggestion in this book. That's to be expected. Try out a few ideas that seem most helpful, given your current strengths and weaknesses.

Experience suggests that though we cannot do everything, we can always do something.

Decide right now that you want a full, rich education, the kind of education that goes beyond merely getting a job and degree (as important as they may be). Getting a degree is not the same thing as getting an education. All around us we see "college educated" experts dumping garbage into our waterways, robbing people of their pensions, or just being dissatisfied and unhappy. Sadly, not every college graduate is well-educated.

You will discover that when your focus shifts from just getting a grade and a degree to developing skills and learning to appreciate things of substance, your whole attitude becomes more receptive to learning. Grades do count, but they're not all that counts.

It's easy to forget that this is your education. Customize it. Work at it. By enrolling in college, you are accepting a personal invitation to participate in "the great conversation." Socrates guided others out of the cave of ignorance, but they provided the effort. I hope this "map" helps you on your way "out of the cave." The next steps are up to you.

> Say not, "When I have leisure I will study." Perhaps you will have no leisure.—Hillel

Appendix A

Simplified Style Guide
for Excellent Papers

Here's a simplified style guide that should be sufficient for most introductory-level philosophy papers and essays. It is loosely based on Joseph Gibaldi's *MLA Handbook for Writers of Research Papers*. Word to the wise: Check with your instructor before you use any style guide.

- **Handwritten papers.** Standard size (8 1/2 × 11 inches), wide-lined notebook paper. Use black or dark blue ink. Write on one side of the page. Do not use sheets torn out of a spiral-bound notebook. For margins, use the ruled lines provided on most lined notebook paper.

- **Typed papers and essays.** Standard size (8 1/2 × 11 inches), heavy paper. Do not use onionskin or easy-erase paper; they smudge. Use a good, black ribbon. Do not use all-italic or other specialized typefaces; use standard Pica or Elite type.

- **Word processors.** Same format as typed paper. For word processing, choose 10- or 12-point standard font. The printer should be set on highest quality (not draft) mode. Do not right-justify or center the body of your text.

- **Double-space all typed or printed text.** Some instructors prefer that you skip every other ruled line for handwritten papers, others do not. Check with yours.

- **Use only one side of the page.**

- **Do not use fancy type.** Use a conventional (Roman) typeface. Do not use script or italics for the body of your text. Use italics (or underlining) for titles, or when quoting italicized material. In formal academic writing, you should avoid italics, boldface, and exclamation points. Let the power and quality of your writing provide the emphasis you want to convey.

- **Margins.** One inch, top, bottom, and both sides, with the exception of page numbers, which are placed 1/2 inch from the top of the page and flush with right margin.

- **Name and course information.** You do not need a title page for a research paper or essay—unless your instructor prefers one. Put your name 1 inch from the top and flush with the left margin on the first page of your paper or essay. Under your name, type your instructor's name, the course name and number, and the date, flush with the left margin.

- **Title.** Center the title three or four lines down from the date. Double-space between the title and the first line of text. Do not italicize (or underline) or put quotation marks around your title. You should, however, italicize (or underline) any words in the title that you would italicize or underline elsewhere in the text, such as the titles of books. If you were writing about Descartes' Meditations, for example, you would italicize (or underline) *Meditations* because that is the title of the book you are writing about. The first lines of the first page of your essay would look something like this:

Ima Happy
Professor Wyse
Introduction to Philosophy 101
March 27, 2006

An Analysis of Descartes' Meditations

In this essay I will show that Cartesian dualism is inconsistent with

the experiences of most people. First,

- **Page numbers.** Do not number the title page. Beginning with page two, number all pages consecutively; upper right-hand corner, 1/2 inch from the top and flush with the right margin. Type only your last name before each page number. Leave one or two spaces between your name and the page number. Use Arabic numerals (1, 2, 3, etc.).

Do not use "p" as an abbreviation for "page," and do not use a hyphen, period, or any other mark or symbol. Here's a sample page 2:

> Pesavento 2
>
> and consequently and indubitably I have established that

- **Paragraphs.** Indent the first line of all paragraphs five spaces or 1/2 inch. Double-space as usual between paragraphs—do not leave extra space.

- **Extended quotations.** If a quote runs more than three lines, indent the entire quote ten spaces (or 1 inch) from the left margin, and cite your source. If it runs less than three lines, embed it in the text (don't forget quotation marks), and cite your source.

- **Fasteners.** Unless your instructor tells you otherwise, staple or paper-clip your paper together in the upper left hand corner, after checking to see which, if either, your professor prefers. Unless explicitly told otherwise, do not use binders or covers, since a stack of them can be cumbersome for instructors to cart around, and binders and covers can make it difficult to write editorial comments on your paper. Never, ever use the old "fold, tear, and pinch" method—unless specifically instructed to do so.

- **Corrections and insertions.** Always proofread your work carefully in time to make corrections. If you are using a word processor, correct the mistake and then reprint the entire page. If you are not using a word processor—and if your instructor allows—insert brief, neatly printed corrections immediately above the error using a caret (∧). Do not use margins to make corrections. Do not make corrections below the lines. Never make more than one or two small corrections per page, and never make corrections on more than two pages of papers less than four pages long. Consult your instructor regarding longer papers.

- **Do not expect your instructor, or the college, to provide you with staples, paper-clips, printers, paper, and so forth.** It is your responsibility to have your paper completely finished and ready to hand in by the date and time your instructor specifies.

- **If you are planning to use the college's computer or writing lab to write your paper, check out lab schedules and computer availability right away.** If necessary, sign up for ample computer time. Budget time for emergencies and computer problems.

- **If you are hiring a typist, allow plenty of time to proofread, and, if necessary, retype the final draft.** Be very clear with the typist regarding how much time he or she will need. Begin lining up a good typist early, and stay in touch once you find one. Remember that no matter who helps you type your paper, you are the one responsible for fulfilling all requirements—and you're the one getting graded.

- **If you are using a word processor, save, save, save, and back up, back up, back up.** Save your work regularly as you type, and always keep two sets of your files—a working disk and a backup disk or CD. It's also a good idea to give a different name to each draft or version of your work in progress. One way to do this is to use the date (Plato 8.14.06) or a sequential alpha or numeric suffix (Plato 1, Plato 2, Plato A, Plato B). Never work on your only copy of a file. If possible, keep copies of your disks in separate places.

CITATIONS

Acknowledge all direct quotes and paraphrases of others' ideas by keying brief parenthetical citations in your text to an alphabetical list of works cited that follows the text. Citations allow scholars and interested readers to verify your research, to get additional information, or to build upon your work. Scrupulous citing is a hallmark of ethical and competent scholarship. Be sure, then, to cite all sources in such a way that a curious reader could, if she or he wished, consult them directly. To that end, scholars follow certain conventions (stylistic arrangements) for documenting source material. The three most common are MLA (Modern Language Association), APA (American Psychological Association), and *Chicago Manual of Style* (Chicago or Turabian, after Kate L. Turabian). MLA and Chicago are widely used in many areas of specialization. APA is favored for scientifically oriented articles. Check to see if your instructor prefers one of these, or another, citation format. Whatever format you use, be sure to include the following: author's name, title, publication information, and date.

- **In-text citations.** Increasingly, scholars use in-text citations rather than endnotes or footnotes for essays and research papers, for modest works, or for work aimed at general audiences, although endnotes and footnotes are also still widely used. Be sure to check with each of your instructors to see which format is required for each of your courses.

The following overview of the in-text citation format provides enough detail for most undergraduate philosophy writing assignments. Minimal information is given in the in-text citation. Complete bibliographic information is provided in a list of works cited, which will be explained below. If your work is more sophisticated, your library and bookstore should have a selection of helpful style and research guides.

As a rule, in-text citations following the MLA format only include the author's last name and page number in the text (Fetters 123). If you are presenting time-sensitive scientific research, the date should be noted as part of the parenthetical in-text citation (Vargas, 1997, p. 88). The Fetters example conforms to MLA style and the Vargas example conforms to APA style for books.

When citing sources that do not indicate who the author is, substitute a short version of the title containing a key word or two. If two or more authors have the same last name, use first initials.

Be sure to document all quotations and paraphrases. Unless instructed otherwise, you should be safe using the modified MLA format described in this appendix. The information you use—author's name, shortened titles, etc.—is determined by your list of works cited.

Always make sure that you understand exactly what format your instructor requires or prefers as soon as you are given any writing assignment. And then follow that format.

CONSTRUCTING A LIST
OF WORKS CITED

Title your list Works Cited, and place it, beginning as a separate, numbered page, at the end of your paper. Center the title Works Cited—1 inch from the top of the page. Double-space. The first line of each citation is put flush with the left margin. Indent the second and subsequent lines five spaces or 1/2 inch. Include all sources: books, articles, online sources, films, CD-ROM sources, and television and radio sources. Proper punctuation is provided in the examples that follow.

■ **Alphabetize.** Arrange all citations (individual entries) alphabetically by author or editor, or title (if no author is identified).

■ **Indent.** Indent (tab) the second and subsequent lines of all entries; keep the first line flush with the left margin.

- **Books by one author.** Author's name, last name first. *Book Title.* Place (city and, if necessary, state) of publisher: Publisher, date. Identify translators or editors after the title. Example:

Jaspers, Karl. *Socrates, Buddha, Confucius, Jesus: The Paradigmatic Individuals,* ed. Hannah Arendt, trans. Ralph Manheim. New York: Harcourt Brace Jovanovich, 1962.

- **Books by two or more authors.** List each author in the order they appear on the title page; reverse the first and last name of the first author only. Example:

Kolak, Daniel, and Raymond Martin. *The Experience of Philosophy.* Belmont, CA: Wadsworth Publishing Company, 1990.

- **Two or more books by the same author.** Give the name for the first entry only. Use three hyphens followed by a period and the title for all subsequent entries (three hyphens stand for "exactly the same name as the name for the preceding entry"). Examples:

Soccio, Douglas J. *Archetypes of Wisdom: An Introduction to Philosophy,* Sixth Edition. Belmont, CA: Wadsworth Publishing Company, 2007.

---. *How to Get the Most Out of Philosophy,* Sixth Edition.Belmont, CA: Wadsworth Publishing Company, 2007.

---, and Vincent F. Barry. *Practical Logic: An Antidote to Uncritical Thinking,* Fifth Edition. Fort Worth, TX: Harcourt Brace, 1998.

- **Books by corporate authors.** Commissions, associations, committees, and any other group whose individual members are not identified are treated as "corporate authors." (Sometimes, the publisher is also the corporate author.) Example:

American Medical Association. *The American Medical Association Encyclopedia of Medicine.* New York: Random House, 1989.

- **Titles.** *Italicize* (or <u>underline</u>) all book, pamphlet, periodical, CD-ROM, and diskette titles. Put magazine and journal article titles in "quotation" marks. Treat individual articles from CD-ROM and diskette sources like magazine and journal article titles by setting them off in quotation marks.

- **Cities.** You do not need to list states or countries for such well-known cities as London, Chicago, San Francisco, Copenhagen, Mexico City, or Paris. You do need to list states or countries for lesser-known cities: Belmont, CA; Herkimer, NY; Brunswick, MO. When two or more cities share the same name, give additional information for the less well known: Cairo, IL; Paris, TX. When two or more cities are equally well known, give additional information for each: Cambridge, UK; Cambridge, MA.

- **Articles in periodicals.** Author. "Article Title." *Magazine or Journal Title* volume number (date): inclusive page numbers.

For newspapers: Author. "Article Title." Newspaper Name (as it appears on the masthead) Date Month Year: Page(s). If the name of the city is not given for a local paper, insert it after the name in square brackets [ ], but don't italicize (or underline) it. If the newspaper prints more than one edition (early, late, national, and so forth), add a comma after the date and give the edition.

Abbreviate the names of every month except May, June, and July. If the paper contains sections (A, B, C, D), include them as part of the first page number. Here are some examples of periodical sources:

Borst, Missy. "Teaching Is My Life." *California Bugle* [Fillmore] 20 Feb. 1971: D6–9.

Gilmar, Sybil T. "Language Foreign to U. S. School," Editorial. *Philadelphia Inquirer* 25 Apr. 1990: A17.

Godfrey, Emma Raym. "But Of Course," Letter. *Chicago Tribune* (June 19, 2006) sec. 4:2.

Hickerdoodle, Cris-Gina. "What Ever Became of Human Nature?" *Computers and the Social Sciences* 14 (1996): 118–123.

Joelson, J. R. "English: The Language of Liberty." *The Humanist* July/Aug. (1989): 35–38.

Malone, Midgetta. "Crediting the Amanuensis: When Proofreading Becomes an Act of Creation." *Riverside Philophaster* 14 Aug. 1945, natl. ed.: A1.

- **CD-ROMs, diskettes, and magnetic tapes.** CD-ROMs, diskettes, and magnetic tapes are sometimes referred to as portable databases for the obvious reason that they can be easily transported and consulted. When citing portable databases be sure to identify the publication medium (CD-ROM, diskette, magnetic tape), the vendor's name, and the date of electronic publication. This information is necessary because there may be different versions of a data source, each with the same title. Because there are so many different configurations of portable databases, you should consult your instructor, or a more complete style guide, if you are unfamiliar with this form of citation. Examples:

American Heritage Dictionary. Microsoft Bookshelf. 1993 ed. CD-ROM. Redmond, WA: Microsoft, 1993.

Carter, J. Scott. "Truman's Legacy of Responsibility." *Carter's PoliSci DataSource.* Magnetic tape. Trinity, CA: Serfdom, 1996.

CIA World Factbook. CD-ROM. Minneapolis: Quanta, 1992.

Hinshaw, Carl Rogers. *Stress: The Student's Friend.* Vers. 1a. Diskette. Clarence Psychological Resources, 1995.

Oxford English Dictionary. 2nd, Ed. CD-ROM. Oxford: Oxford University Press, 1992.

Where in the World Is Carmen Sandiego? Deluxe ed. CD-ROM. Novato, CA: Brøderbund, 1992.

- **Online sources.** Online databases are "intangible" in the sense that you cannot buy them, store them, or carry them with you. They are often large, and regularly modified and updated. It can be difficult, if not impossible, to be sure that the material available at a given time is the same as it was when previously consulted. Consequently, data from online sources requires careful scrutiny (as, of course, do all sources). Also, online data is considered "published," or unique, whenever it is posted or modified. Thus, online citations must always include the publication medium, computer service or network, and access date.

- **Publication medium.** Identify your source medium as online.

- **Name of computer service or network.** Infotrac, Lexis-Nexis, ERIC, and Hippias are examples of computer services. The Internet is a vast computer network; as such, the Internet is inadequate as a citation source without other information, so be sure to provide the name of the server or website address of your source.

- **Access date.** Because each online "publication" is considered unique, you may have to list more than one date, particularly if you are citing a source originally published in another medium, such as a magazine or newspaper. A complete citation will include the hard copy date and the online date.

- **Examples of online source citations.**
Alston, Robin. "The Battle of the Books." *Humanist* 7.0176 (10 Sept. 1993): 10 pp. Online. Internet. 10 Oct. 1993.

"Middle Ages." *Academic American Encyclopedia.* Online. Prodigy. 30 Mar. 1992.

Shakespeare, William. *Hamlet. The Works of William Shakespeare.* Ed. Arthur H. Bullen. Stratford Town Ed. Stratford-on-Avon: Shakespeare Head, 1911. Online. Dartmouth College Library. Internet. 26 Dec. 1992.

> This is a simplified style guide. Be sure your instructor approves of its use. Better yet, invest in your education by purchasing your own copy of a good style guide. Ask your instructors for recommendations or see the bibliography at the end of this book.

A SAMPLE WORKS CITED

This sample contains all of the preceding examples, arranged alphabetically.

Works Cited

Alston, Robin. "The Battle of the Books." *Humanist* 7.0176 (10 Sept. 1993): 10 pp. Online. Internet. 10 Oct. 1993.

American Heritage Dictionary. Microsoft Bookshelf. 1993 ed. CD-ROM. Redmond, WA: Microsoft, 1993.

American Medical Association. *The American Medical Association Encyclopedia of Medicine.* New York: Random House, 1989.

Borst, Missy. "Teaching Is My Life." *California Bugle* [Fillmore] 20 Feb. 1971: D6–9.

Carter, J. Scott. "Truman's Legacy of Responsibility." *Carter's PoliSci DataSource.* Magnetic tape. Trinity, CA: Serfdom, 1996.

CIA World Factbook. CD-ROM. Minneapolis: Quanta, 1992.

Gilmar, Sybil T. "Language Foreign to U. S. School," Editorial. *Philadelphia Inquirer* 25 Apr. 1990: A17.

Godfrey, Emma Raym. "But Of Course," Letter. *Chicago Tribune* (June 19, 2006) sec. 4:2.

Hickerdoodle, Cris-Gina. "What Ever Became of Human Nature?" *Computers and the Social Sciences* 14 (1996): 118–123.

Hinshaw, Carl Rogers. *Stress: The Student's Friend.* Vers. 1a. Diskette. Clarence Psychological Resources, 1995.

Jaspers, Karl. *Socrates, Buddha, Confucius, Jesus: The Paradigmatic Individuals,* ed. Hannah Arendt, trans. Ralph Manheim. New York: Harcourt Brace Jovanovich, 1962.

Joelson, J. R. "English: The Language of Liberty." *The Humanist* July/Aug. (1989): 35–38.

Kolak, Daniel, and Raymond Martin. *The Experience of Philosophy.* Belmont, CA: Wadsworth Publishing Company, 1990.

Malone, Midgetta. "Crediting the Amanuensis: When Proofreading Becomes an Act of Creation." *Riverside Philophaster* 14 Aug. 1945, natl. ed.: A1.

"Middle Ages." *Academic American Encyclopedia.* Online. Prodigy. 30 Mar. 1992.

Oxford English Dictionary. 2nd, Ed. CD-ROM. Oxford: Oxford University Press, 1992.

Shakespeare, William. *Hamlet. The Works of William Shakespeare.* Ed. Arthur H. Bullen. Stratford Town Ed. Stratford-on-Avon: Shakespeare Head, 1911. Online. Dartmouth College Library. Internet. 26 Dec. 1992.

Soccio, Douglas J. *Archetypes of Wisdom: An Introduction to Philosophy,* Sixth Edition. Belmont, CA: Wadsworth Publishing Company, 2007.

---. *How to Get the Most Out of Philosophy,* Sixth Edition. Belmont, CA: Wadsworth Publishing Company, 2007.

---, and Vincent E. Barry. *Practical Logic: An Antidote to Uncritical Thinking,* Fifth Edition. Fort Worth, TX: Harcourt Brace, 1998.

Where in the World is Carmen Sandiego? Deluxe ed. CD-ROM. Novato, CA: Brøderbund, 1992.

Appendix B

Test Taking

Before the gates of excellence, the high gods have placed sweat.
HESIOD

Though it may not always seem like it, tests are designed to see what you have learned in a particular course, not what you don't know. Fortunately, there are basic guidelines for maximizing your chances of doing well on any kind of test. This section covers basic test preparation and specific tips for essay, short-answer, and objective tests.

PREPARING FOR TESTS

- **STUDY, STUDY, STUDY.** The single best preparation for any kind of test is practicing effective study habits on a routine basis.

- **Take advantage of "free" tests and quizzes.** If your instructor offers extra-credit tests, or drops one or more tests, be sure to take every test. Dropped or extra-credit tests amount to free practice.

- **Be sure to attend any test reviews.** Some instructors devote the class period preceding a test to last-minute questions and review. Be sure to take advantage of such an opportunity by coming to class with written questions.

- **Study as if all tests are essay tests—whether they are or not.** Studies have shown that students perform worse when they gear their studying to objective tests. In one experiment, one group of students was told to prepare for an essay test, but actually given an objective test. Another group of students was told to prepare for, and actually given, an objective test. The students who had been expecting an essay test did markedly better. This pattern has been confirmed many times. (See below for specific advice on studying for essay tests.)

■ **Avoid cramming.** Although some students insist that they learn best under pressure, research suggests caution. Too much anxiety interferes with critical thinking skills and other cognitive abilities. Memory retention markedly declines, the ability to reason diminishes, even perceptual skills decrease under extreme anxiety and stress. Also, skills classes require regular practice. Courses such as logic, critical thinking, most science, and all math courses cover both information and skills, so cramming cannot compensate for regular, incremental studying.

■ **Get your normal amount of sleep the night before the test.** Fatigue produces and exacerbates some of the same conditions as anxiety: impaired retention of information, "processing errors" (misreading, spelling mistakes, filling in the wrong part of the exam, overlooking key instructions), and diminished thinking skills. Sleep deprivation can also trigger depression and other "down" emotions, which interfere with testing well.

■ **Study under conditions similar to actual testing conditions.** For example, avoid drinking caffeinated drinks while you study unless you are sure you can drink them during or right before the exam. Studies show that students have a much higher rate of retrieving information when their biochemical state is the same as when they learned it: Students who sipped coffee while studying did better on tests when they were allowed to sip coffee during the test than when they weren't.

■ **Eat wisely before the test.** Don't eat a big meal or candy bar right before the test. The last thing you want to experience during a test is that drowsy feeling that can follow a big meal. But do eat and drink (nonalcoholic beverages) lightly before the test. When your blood sugar is too low during a test, you can feel shaky, weak, and confused. You can also be confused if you're severely dehydrated.

■ **Allow extra time to get to class on test day.** Again, do all that you can to avoid disruptive anxiety. Get to class early enough to select your usual seat; make sure you have any necessary pens, pencils, paper, bluebooks, machine-scored answer sheets, and notes (if allowed).

VERY IMPORTANT TIP: Always pick up your graded tests and attend class the days graded tests are discussed. Your grade is not the only thing that matters when it comes to taking tests. Learning from mistakes and correcting errors always pays off on subsequent tests, even when the tested topics vary. Collecting and studying each and every test is the first step in preparing for future tests.

RELAXATION TECHNIQUES
FOR BETTER TEST SCORES

Practice the following relaxation techniques—especially if you tend to panic on tests:

- **Stretch slowly and leisurely before taking your seat.**

- **Remind yourself that your performance on the test, no matter how important, does not measure your worth as a human being, or predict your chances of finding ultimate happiness.**

- **Remind yourself that you are already a test-taking expert.** You've already taken hundreds, if not thousands, of tests in grade school and high school, perhaps in the military or applying for jobs.

- **Take a tip from successful athletes and performers: Visualize yourself taking the test and doing well.** Creative visualization is not the same thing as vaguely imagining something. Visualization is not a dreamy fantasy, but a detailed, focused, highly concentrated, carefully structured, step-by-step mental imaging of a future event; in this case, the test. Sports and performance psychologists report that creative visualization can enhance the effectiveness of prepared and capable athletes and performers in a variety of fields. Visualization is not a substitute for solid preparation.

- **Practice deep breathing.** Force yourself to breathe deeply and slowly, especially when you are nervous and your natural inclination is to hyperventilate.

- **Immediately after you receive the test, put your pencil down, put the test face down, close your eyes, place both hands on the desk, and breathe slowly and deeply for a few seconds.** Tell yourself that you will do well. These few seconds can save you from rushing into the test in a state of unproductive anxiety.

- **Then slowly turn your test over, slowly read it through, slowly pick up your pencil, and go to work.** Consciously avoid the kind of jerky, "hyper" movements associated with panic or fear. Such movements can reinforce and stimulate panic or fear. Monitor your breathing, too. When you feel panicked, put your pencil down and breathe deeply for a few seconds.

- **Be thankful for a touch of anxiety.** Clinical studies have shown that a bit of anxiety can be an advantage because moderately heightened adrenal function (short of a panic level) increases cognitive and perceptual acuity. Some anxiety is normal and usually helpful.

> Deal with it before it is there; check disorder before it is rife.
> Deal with the hard while it is still easy, the great while it is still small.
> —Lao-tzu

HOW TO DO YOUR BEST
ON ESSAY TESTS

- **Read the whole test before answering any questions.**

- **Follow all instructions.** Note the time limit, if any. Note if you must answer all questions or only some. Pay attention to the relative value of questions.

- **Familiarize yourself with all questions before answering any.** This will allow you to organize a strategy for getting the most correct answers. Further, reading one question might remind you of the answer to a different question.

- **First answer the questions you know the most about.** Don't worry if these questions aren't worth as much as other questions. Beginning from strength has a number of advantages: You can get right to work, thus maximizing your time. You're sure to have some correct answers. You'll boost your confidence and reduce anxiety. You'll kick your mind into gear quickly and avoid the panic and confusion that can result from wrestling with a question that draws a blank.

- **When in doubt, write.** If you can't think of anything to write about any question, write something about one of them anyway. On scratch paper preferably (if scratch paper is allowed), write down

113

anything you can remember that's even remotely connected to the question. If you keep writing, you'll probably discover information, connections, and patterns that seemed beyond reach. You may have to scrap most of this "creative" writing once your mind kicks into gear, and write a more polished essay, but that's all right.

- **Neatness counts.** Your instructor should not have to decipher bad handwriting, decode crossed-out passages, or convoluted arrows connecting a sentence on page two to a sentence on page four. If you must make extensive corrections to an essay answer, completely and clearly cross out the undesired work. Ask the instructor or proctor if you can begin on a new sheet of paper, if necessary.

- **If you are responsible for providing your own bluebooks or paper, be sure to have plenty of the kind specified.** Some instructors require their students to bring in bluebooks a class period or two before the test. They then check to ensure that the bluebooks are blank, and may stamp or sign them to indicate this. Allow ample time to buy your bluebooks and take extra precautions not to fold or wrinkle them. Your instructor may refuse to grade a test written on unapproved paper or in an unapproved bluebook.

- **Never use your own paper without asking, and don't go fishing around through your notebook or backpack for paper, pens, or anything else.** You might know you're not cheating, but your instructor might not.

- **Use complete sentences; don't use abbreviations unless explicitly informed that you may; use good grammar.** Essay tests ask for essays, not collections of fragmentary notes. Bad grammar is almost always associated with cloudy thinking. At the very least, bad grammar weakens your ideas.

- **Spell all technical terms and proper names correctly.** There is absolutely no excuse for not learning how to spell the important terms that are introduced as part of a course. This applies to terms derived from Greek, Latin, and other languages that are difficult for you. The fact that a word is unusual or hard to pronounce just means that you have to work a little harder to become comfortable with it.

- **On essay and short-answer tests, mention specific relevant examples, persons, titles, and terms from assigned readings, the textbook, and the instructor's lectures.** Be specific. Show that you are knowledgeable in terms of this class. Essay tests have two functions: to show that you can think on a sophisticated level and to show that you have acquired new information.

Your essays should always present relevant, significant information in a coherent fashion.

■ **Make and show connections; don't just list facts and information.** Avoid the extremes of the overly general essay that does not reveal an adequate fund of information, and the "pseudo-essay" that is so crammed with facts that it is not a coherent essay at all.

■ **Make sure to answer the question that is asked.** Pay attention to such instructions as "compare and contrast," "explain why," "analyze," and so forth. Follow instructions. Your instructor may not give credit for wonderful insights, no matter how brilliantly expressed, if they are not responsive to the question as it is framed.

■ **Don't combine questions.** Even if the answers to two or three questions overlap, it's best to answer each question separately and answer it exactly as it is asked. Don't mentally "reword" questions. Grading essays is hard work, and most instructors will find evaluating combined questions especially difficult, because even closely related questions require different emphases.

■ **Keep track of the time.** Don't try to write perfect essays. You might spend too much time on one or two questions. Allow time for a quick scan of all your answers at the end of the testing period so you can catch any glaring errors or omissions.

■ **Answer every required question.** Partial credit (no matter how little) is far better than no credit. Your instructor has good reasons for the combination of questions included on your test, so don't defeat them by avoiding required questions. It is not wise to answer "extra" questions to "compensate" for not answering one or more required questions. This never works. Trying to get away with this evasion is tantamount to your mechanic adjusting your brakes when you have a steering problem because he's unable to fix the steering.

■ **Reread your answer before turning it in.** Consider proofreading your answer as a vital part of writing it. It may be tempting (and common) to write up to the last second, but it is more effective not to have to. This is another reason to be very well prepared for the test: You will be able to start writing right away, and will have many valuable things to say.

■ **Write a clear conclusion that uses key phrases and examples from your essay.** A lucid, focused conclusion encourages your reader to look more favorably on your essay than just stopping in the middle of.

■ **Be sure you have put your name on your test.**

HOW TO DO YOUR BEST
ON COMPLETION TESTS

■ **Read the entire test before answering any questions.** Later questions may contain useful information for answering earlier questions, and vice versa. Reading the entire test gives you the "lay of the land," so you can maximize your time by first going quickly through questions you know very well, and then concentrating on more complex or difficult questions.

■ **Follow instructions.** This is always important, but it is crucial when tests are scored by teaching assistants or student aides who may not have the expertise or authority to deal with improvisations or modifications of the requested format.

■ **Use the kind of pen or pencil required, and be very careful when you fill in your answers or erase them.** It is difficult and tiring to read light, brightly colored inks and very light (hard) pencil lead. You should always use black or blue ink or a No. 1 or No. 2 pencil, unless your instructor specifies otherwise.

■ **Spell technical terms and proper names correctly. Do not abbreviate. Always assume spelling counts.**

■ **Write legibly.**

■ **Confine your answers to the space allowed.** If you are allowed to use additional space, mark your continuations very clearly. Always ask before assuming you can use additional space.

■ **Pay attention to key words and phrases; underline them if you're allowed to.** Key words include qualifiers like always, never, usually, mostly, sometimes, not, in part, and without exception. Watch for important qualifiers like "according to the text," or "in lecture."

■ **Answer every question.** In most cases, you will be graded on the number of correct answers (check to be sure). A blank and a wrong answer are both worth zero. You have nothing to lose by writing something (and you may be correct and not know it). You might get partial credit.

■ **Don't waste time dwelling on difficult questions.** Keep going, and come back to difficult questions after you've made one complete pass through the test.

■ **Review the test before you turn it in.** The review process does more than catch omissions and errors; it can also trigger answers that were just out of reach before.

■ **Don't forget to put your name on your test.**

HOW TO DO YOUR BEST
ON OBJECTIVE TESTS

■ **Read the entire test before answering any questions.** Later questions may contain useful information for answering earlier questions, and vice versa. Reading the entire test gives you the "lay of the land," so you can maximize your time by first going quickly through questions you know very well, and then concentrating on more complex or difficult questions.

■ **Follow instructions.** This is always important, but it is crucial when tests are machine scored.

■ **If your test will be machine scored, use the kind of pen or pencil required, and be very careful when you fill in your answers or erase them.** The most common grading machines are made to read clearly defined, heavy black pencil markings. The safest kind of pencil to use is the "No. 2" type. No. 2 grade lead is soft enough to make a dark mark, but hard enough not to smudge. Some machines require special pencils.

■ **If you are responsible for providing your own machine-scored answer sheets, be sure to bring two or three forms of the kind specified.** Allow ample time to buy your answer sheets, and take extra precautions not to fold or wrinkle them. Your instructor may refuse to grade an answer sheet that cannot be read by the grading machine.

■ **Answer the easiest questions first.** You want to score as many correct answers as quickly as possible. Also, the positive experience of providing correct answers will boost your confidence, minimize test anxiety, and probably help you recall the answers to some of the questions that you did not answer initially.

■ **If all questions are of equal weight, don't dawdle over difficult questions until you have made one complete pass through the test.**

■ **Pay attention to key words and phrases; underline them if you're allowed to.** Key words include qualifiers like: always, never, usually, mostly, sometimes, not, in part, without exception. Watch for important qualifiers like "according to the text," or "in lecture."

■ **On true-false questions, pay special attention to universal terms like "always," "all," and "never."** Such terms allow for no exceptions. If you're not sure of the answer to a question containing universal qualifiers, your best guess is false.

117

- **Do not look for patterns among the answers; answer each question independently.** Don't worry, for example, about how many "true" or how many "C" answers there are. It is quite possible that by accident or diabolical instructor scheming all the answers are true or C—or no answer is C, or true.

- **If a question seems utterly unintelligible or lacking any correct answer, ask your instructor for clarification.** The worst that can happen is that you're told that the question is correct. Then you can rethink it or go on to questions you can answer. But you might be right. Tests do contain errors.

- **On multiple-choice questions, mentally turn each choice into a true-false question.** The leading statement plus the correct choice always yields a true statement (assuming only one correct answer). After you've chosen an answer, read the leading statement plus your choice to see if they produce a true statement. Here's a simple example:

> 10. Plato was the pupil of _____ and the teacher of _____.
>   A. Aristotle, Socrates
>   B. Diogenes, Socrates
>   C. Socrates, Aristotle
>   D. Aristotle, Alexander the Great
>   E. None of these.

The correct answer is C. If we add C to the leading statement, we get: "Plato was the pupil of Socrates and the teacher of Aristotle." This is a true statement. No other choice produces a true statement when added to the leading statement.

- **On multiple-choice questions, always choose the most precise correct answer if more than one choice is correct.** If you are expected to select the "best" option on multiple-choice questions, it helps to think of selecting one option as rejecting the other options. Here's an example from a logic test to help illustrate this point. In this class, *an argument is defined as a group of propositions, one of which (the conclusion) is claimed to follow logically from other propositions (premises).* Which answer would you select as the "best" answer based on the italicized definition?

> 28. An argument consists of _____.
>   A. a group of propositions
>   B. at least one premise
>   C. a conclusion
>   D. A, B, and C
>   E. None of these.

Congratulations if you picked D; it's the "best" answer. A, B, and C are each "correct" in the sense that an argument does contain a group of propositions (A), one of which is the conclusion (C), and one of which is a premise (B). The problem with picking A, B, or C is a function of the nature of multiple-choice questions: Picking the one best multiple-choice option has the effect of denying all of the other options. This is easily illustrated by analyzing exactly what's involved with picking option A. Picking option A amounts to saying this: "An argument consists of *a group of propositions,* but not at least one premise and not a conclusion." Picking B amounts to saying: "An argument consists of *a minimum of one premise,* but not a group of propositions and not a conclusion." Picking C amounts to saying: "An argument consists of *a conclusion,* but not a group of propositions and not at least one premise." Picking E is the worst possible answer.

■ **Answer each question exactly as it is worded; don't "mentally correct" or rewrite it.** It is unfortunately quite common for test takers to ignore key words or phrases in questions, or to "mentally correct" them.

Here's an example of mentally "correcting" a question: I once assigned a random ID number to students to use in posting grades. The syllabus (that had been given to each student the first day of class) stated, "You must put your random ID number on all tests, once you have been assigned a number. NO ASSIGNMENTS WILL BE GRADED WITHOUT THIS NUMBER." The second week of class I gave a test over the course syllabus. I had not yet assigned random numbers. One of the true-false questions was "You must put your random ID number on all tests." Every student picked true. The correct answer was false. To be true the statement would have to be amended as follows: "You must put your random ID number on all tests, once you have been assigned a number."

The class accused me of being "nit picky" and unfair. I pointed out that the statement was obviously false since no one was required to use a random number on this very test! I explained that since this was a test for which a random number was not required, the statement "You must put your random ID number on all tests" had to be false. Quite a few students said something like this: "I figured you didn't mean this test. I figured you meant once we have our numbers. . . ." In other words, those students modified the wording of the question; they mentally altered it according to their own ideas of what it should have been.

> Don't mentally add or delete words or phrases to questions. You might do this without being aware of it. Next time you are going over a corrected test, be alert for this tendency. See if you are inadvertently altering the questions from their actual wording.

- **Change answers only if you have good reasons.** Statistically, more students change from correct answers to incorrect ones than change from incorrect to correct ones, but not always. Think twice if you find yourself tempted to change lots of answers, but don't be afraid to change an answer if you have a good reason to.

- **Double-check your answer sheet before turning it in.** Make sure you've used the proper kind of pen or pencil and erased cleanly. Count your answers and check to see if you've skipped a line or put two answers on one line.

- **Be sure your name is on your answer sheet (and your test, if required).**

HOW TO DO YOUR BEST
ON COMBINATION TESTS

- **On tests containing more than one kind of question, first scan the entire test, and then answer questions in this order: multiple-choice first, true-false second, completion third, and essay last—regardless of the order in which they occur on your test.** Multiple-choice questions provide a selective review of material, without requiring the cold recollection of completion questions or the tantalizing seductiveness of true-false questions. Multiple-choice questions provide information and trigger recall for the prepared student.

- **Take your time, but don't dawdle; you'll want to allow time to reread and change answers.**

- **Don't dwell on questions that are not worth very many points.** Having read the entire test before answering any questions helps you budget your time according to the relative weight of each section.

- **Be sure you understand the rules for matching-type questions.** Can the same choice be used to match more than one item?

Must every choice be used? Be very clear on these conditions. If they are not stated on the test, ask your instructor.

- **As always, reread your answers before turning in your test.**
- **Remember your best bet is to study as if all tests are essay tests.**
- **Review the previous material pertaining to specific kinds of tests.**
- **Be sure your name is on your test.**

Appendix C

Letters of Recommendation

As I learned during my sophomore year in college (see Preface), it is difficult for most instructors to write a persuasive letter of recommendation based only on a student's grades. The most effective letters of recommendation refer to your unique qualities. Get to know three or four instructors well enough for them to recommend you personally.

As the term implies, a letter of recommendation is a written evaluation attesting to your abilities and recommending you for favorable consideration as a candidate for scholarships, financial aid, admissions to academic and vocational programs, or a job. Letters of recommendation may be sent directly to those requesting them, or they may be held by your college's placement office, in a file known as a *dossier*. Your dossier will also contain your current transcript. Check to see if your school offers dossier service. The great advantage of having a dossier on file is that you don't need to ask for letters over and over, and you don't have to worry about losing track of them. Also, your instructor may no longer be at the college if you request a letter some time after you've completed the course. Once you have established a dossier, it is easy to have your dossier sent to whomever receives your job or school application. The placement office, or whichever office provides the service, mails out official copies of your dossier for a modest handling fee. You can add to your dossier as you get more letters of recommendation.

Because they free their writers to be very candid, the most effective letters of recommendation are not seen by their subjects. Don't be disturbed if you don't get to see your letters. If you are afraid of getting a negative evaluation from a professor, do not ask him or her for a letter. If you are given the choice between a letter you will be allowed to read or a "blind" letter, the blind letter may be a better bet because it will be interpreted as being more thorough than a letter written with the knowledge that you will read it.

The most effective letters of recommendation are written by individuals with the training and experience to recognize superior merit or promise. They are personalized, and are based on sufficient relevant contact with you and your work. Keep this in mind when choosing people to write your letters of recommendation.

The time to deal with letters of recommendation is immediately. Even if you aren't sure you'll need any, play it safe and assume that you will. It can be difficult to write effective recommendations for students years after they've taken a course. With that in mind, here's a strategy for getting good letters of recommendation. This strategy pays off in other ways, too.

No matter what your present goals are, proceed with the assumption that at some point in your life you will need letters of recommendation from at least three of your professors.

- **Drop by and just say hello.** Stop by and introduce yourself to your professors early in the term. You don't have to make a production of it or engage in "kissing up." Explain why you're taking the class, what you hope to gain from it, and what your educational plans are.

- **Speak up in class.** Show interest in your courses by being an active participant. Make thoughtful comments—if you are current with your studies.

- **Stop by when things are going well.** Reintroduce yourself, discuss what you've learned, what progress you've made, and so forth. Don't just show up to complain or ask for favors.

- **Perform at a level worthy of an honest recommendation.** Colleges, professional programs, and potential employers look at more than just grades. Your "performance" includes responsibility (Did you meet deadlines? Did you attend class regularly?); reliability (Did you follow instructions? Did you pay attention to details? Did you proofread your papers?); teachability (Did you give new ideas a fair hearing?); maturity (Did you take criticism well and refrain from blaming others for your problems?); citizenship (Were you respectful of others? Did you do your part to make it a good class?); self-motivation (Did you sustain a high level of effort without having to be pushed constantly?); creativity (Did you think for yourself and add your own personal style to your coursework?).

- **Don't be afraid to request a recommendation just because you didn't get an A or B from the professor you want to write it.** Assess your overall performance in light of all relevant factors, not just grades. Although grades tend to be the chief markers of value in academia, other factors count, too. Character matters in college, as in the rest of life. My personal sense of things is that certain personal traits—a good work ethic, a realistic sense of self, modesty, integrity, civility—matter more for long-term well-being than high grades and intellectual cleverness.

- **Don't assume that you can't get a letter of recommendation just because you aren't an A-student—and don't assume that just being an A-student is all that it takes to get a strong recommendation.** There are many kinds of recommendation: purely academic; purely vocational; those that emphasize character or personal growth; most letters are combination letters. The most helpful recommendations combine academic and personal assessment. The surly, difficult A-student is not necessarily more desirable than the eager, hardworking, promising B-student or C-student.

> Don't even think about being a surly, difficult student—unless you are so talented and brilliant that the rest of us will be forced to overlook your unpleasantness. And if you are that brilliant, why not be grateful and gracious as well?

- **Demonstrate commendable character and motivation.** Show up for all classes on time; turn in assignments on time and in the requested format; be polite and work hard.

- **Show that you learn from criticism.** If weaknesses are identified in essays or papers, make sure not to repeat them in subsequent work.

- **Take more than one class from the same professor.** Taking additional courses from the same instructor increases the chances that the instructor will be able to write a strong letter on your behalf. Some instructors will feel uncomfortable writing a letter of recommendation for a student who has only taken one class with them, no matter how well you do in that one class. Classes that involve regular discussion, lots of writing, and office visits are exceptions, because professor-student interaction is an essential and regular part of the class.

- **Request your letter in a timely fashion.** Ask for your letter two or three weeks before you need it.

- **Provide pertinent written information when you make your request.** It's a very good idea to provide a written statement of your plans and goals at the time you ask for a letter of recommendation. Also mention any helpful personal information: Are you a parent? Do you work? Where? How many hours? What's your major? What's your immediate goal (scholarship, four-year transfer, graduate school, and so on)? What's your long-term goal (psychologist, philosopher, preacher, engineer, nurse, forest ranger)?

- **Provide a copy of your transcript and a list of your current courses when you request a letter of recommendation.** Be sure to flag any courses you've taken from the instructor you're asking to write the letter.

- **Choose your letter writers wisely.** Select instructors who know your abilities and can honestly recommend you with enthusiasm. In today's world of inflated recommendations, a mediocre letter can be worse than no letter.

- **Always ask if the professor can comfortably write a strong letter for you.** Too often, today's letters of recommendation are grossly inflated. As embarrassing and disappointing as it can be to learn that your professor doesn't feel that she or he can write a strong recommendation, it's much better to learn that before a weak letter has done its damage.

- **Politely check on your letter's progress in about a week.** Don't hector your professor, but don't just assume that she or he will remember to write your letter. After a week or so, a gentle inquiry is in order.

- **Be sure to get some letters from instructors in courses that are relevant to your future plans.** A letter from your philosophy instructor is not likely to carry as much weight for admissions to a music program as one from your music instructor. Failure to provide relevant letters may arouse concern in those reviewing your application.

- **Don't leave college without at least three letters of recommendation.** Just because you don't plan to continue in school doesn't mean you won't need letters of recommendation. People change their minds. Further, good college recommendations can be used when applying for jobs, admission to police or fire-fighting academies, and special military programs. Potential employers will look for signs of responsibility, ambition, maturity, ability to solve problems, complete a program, and other desirable qualities.

- **If your instructors give you copies of their letters, keep them together in a file—and keep a backup file in a separate safe place.** This is good advice even if you are registered with the school's placement service.

Don't forget to set up a dossier file at your school's placement office.

Beginning Philosopher's Bibliography

There is no such thing as an interesting book,
there are only interested readers.

RALPH WALDO EMERSON

Following are lists of books about writing, thinking, and succeeding in college. I have included focused, brief books that can be read quickly or studied on an as-needed basis, if you wish to supplement the material in this book, as well as more substantial reference sources.

PHILOSOPHICALLY ORIENTED
STUDY BOOKS

Barnet, Sylvan, and Hugo Bedau, eds. *Critical Thinking, Reading, and Writing: A Brief Guide to Argument,* Fifth Edition. Boston: Bedford Books/St. Martin's Press, 2004. This 560-page book includes a good chapter on sources and documentation.

Seech, Zachary. *Writing Philosophy Papers,* Fourth Edition. Belmont, CA: Wadsworth Publishing Company, 2004. An excellent guide to writing philosophy papers, this 152-page text is not only valuable to philosophy students; its contents can be applied to any critical writing assignments.

Woodhouse, Mark B. *A Preface to Philosophy,* Seventh Edition. Belmont, CA: Wadsworth Publishing Company, 2003. This 163-page survey of what philosophy is all about includes a handy glossary of philosophical terms.

PHILOSOPHY REFERENCE BOOKS

Angeles, Peter A. *Dictionary of Philosophy.* New York: Barnes & Noble Books, 1981.

Audi, Robert, ed. *The Cambridge Dictionary of Philosophy,* Second Edition. Cambridge: Cambridge University Press, 1999. This 1039-page comprehensive reference includes entries by 436 philosophers.

Blackburn, Simon. *The Oxford Dictionary of Philosophy.* Oxford: Oxford University Press, 1994. This witty and authoritative philosophical dictionary includes useful cross-references.

Bunnin, Nicholas, and E. P. Tsui-James, eds. *The Blackwell Companion to Philosophy,* Second Edition. Oxford: Blackwell Publishers Ltd., 2002. Although presented as a textbook, this is an excellent reference book for the serious philosopher: technical, thorough, and carefully edited.

Copleston, Frederick, S. J. *A History of Philosophy.* New York: Doubleday, Image edition, 1985. Copleston's strength is his ability to summarize and explain other philosophers' ideas without intruding. His own editorial comments are always clearly identified. This excellent history is available in a cumbersome, but affordable, three-book edition and an easier-to-handle nine-volume series.

Craig, Edward, ed. *The Routledge Encyclopedia of Philosophy.* London: Routledge, 1998. This ten-volume set has been described as the *Oxford English Dictionary* of philosophy. A one-volume, 1077-page Shorter Edition (2005) consists of over 900 entries.

Edwards, Paul, ed. in chief. *The Encyclopedia of Philosophy.* New York: Macmillan & Free Press, 1967. Two versions of this indispensable source are available, the regular edition of eight separate volumes and a four-volume "student edition" that contains exactly the same material. Though some of the articles in the encyclopedia can be difficult for novice philosophers, this is a superb source of general information regarding philosophers and philosophical issues and arguments. A 1996 supplement updates the original.

Honderich, Ted, ed. *The Oxford Companion to Philosophy,* Second Edition. Oxford: Oxford University Press, 2005. Checking in at a massive

1100 pages, Honderich's book is one of the most thorough single-volume reference books available—nearly an encyclopedia.

Mautner, Thomas, ed. *A Dictionary of Philosophy*. Oxford: Blackwell Publishers Ltd., 1996. This dictionary contains entries from more than one hundred distinguished philosophers.

Scharfstein, Ben-Ami. *The Philosophers: Their Lives and the Nature of Their Thought*. Oxford: Oxford University Press, 1989. Scharfstein's little book is a fascinating blend of philosophy, history, and psychology.

Singer, Peter, ed. *A Companion to Ethics*. Oxford: Blackwell Publishers Ltd., 1993. This solid addition to the *Blackwell Companion to Philosophy* series consists of 47 entries written by some of today's leading philosophers; entries include up-to-date bibliographies.

STUDY SKILLS BOOKS

Armstrong, William H. *Study Is Hard Work,* Second Edition. Boston: David R. Godine, 1998. Run to your nearest library or bookstore and grab a copy of this 160-page classic by the author of *Sounder*. Among other things (writing and herding sheep, to mention two), Armstrong taught history for over fifty years. His wise, honest book is sobering and inspiring in that best of ways: It calls on the best in us.

Carey, Stephen S. *A Beginner's Guide to Scientific Method,* Second Edition. Belmont, CA: Wadsworth Publishing Company, 1997. This clearly written 138-page book helps students master the critical thinking skills that are specific to science through the use of entertaining and worthwhile exercises.

Gibbs, J. J. *Dancing With Your Books: The Zen Way of Studying*. New York: Penguin Books, 1990. This 181-page surprise is elegant and soothing, a book worth keeping.

Lunenfeld, Marvin, and Peter Lunenfeld. *College Basics: How to Start Right and Finish Strong,* Second Edition. Buffalo: Semester Press, 1994. This college self-help book, written by a father and his son who are also a professor and a student, packs a lot of useful material into a modest size.

Mundsack, Allan, James Deese, and Ellin K. Deese. *How to Study,* Fifth Edition, Revised. New York: McGraw-Hill, 2002. This 144-page primer is a minor classic with great reading tips.

Robinson, Adam. *What Smart Students Know: Maximum Grades. Optimal Learning*. New York: Three Rivers Press, 1997. Robinson's 288-page book is built on the intriguing premise that there is a world of difference

129

between being a smart person and being a smart student—and shows students of all levels how to be smarter students.

Smith, Richard Manning. *Mastering Mathematics: How to Be a Great Math Student,* Third Edition. Belmont, CA: Brooks Cole Publishing Company, 1999. At 240 pages, this is one of the most effective, specialized how-to books on the market.

Watson, Richard. *Good Teaching: A Guide for Students.* Carbondale and Edwardsville, IL: Southern Illinois University Press, 1997. Watson is a wonderful writer: acerbic, profound, and dead-on honest. This 48-page volume pulls no punches in its charge to students: You are responsible for learning. Watson writes from the unique perspective of being a respected scholar and teacher at a first-rate research university. It's a wise student who listens to advice from "insiders," and Richard Watson is tough, caring, and funny.

EIGHT GUIDES TO BETTER WRITING

Philosophy instructors tend to accept any consistent "commonly used" system of citations. The Chicago (Turabian) and MLA (Modern Language Association) style guides are the most widely used formats for most subject areas. Psychology students may be required to use the APA (American Psychological Association) style for term papers and essays.

American Psychological Association. *The Concise Rules of APA Style.* Washington, DC: American Psychological Association, 2005.

———. *Publication Manual of the American Psychological Association,* Fifth Edition. Washington, DC: American Psychological Association, 2001.

Fulwer, Toby, and Alan R. Hayakawa, *The Blair Handbook,* Third Edition. Englewood Cliffs, NJ: Prentice-Hall, 1999.

Gibaldi, Joseph. *MLA Handbook for Writers of Research Papers,* Sixth Edition. New York: Modern Language Association, 2003.

Harris, Muriel. *Prentice Hall Reference Guide to Grammar and Usage,* Sixth Edition. Englewood Cliffs, NJ: Prentice-Hall, 2000.

Staff of the University of Chicago Press. *Chicago Manual of Style,* 15th Edition. Chicago: University of Chicago Press, 2003.

Strunk, William, Jr., and E. B. White. Maira Kalman, illus. *Elements of Style, Illustrated Edition.* New York: Penguin Press, 2005.

Turabian, Kate L. *A Manual for Writers of Term Papers, Theses, and Dissertations,* Sixth Edition. Revised by John Grossman and Alice Bennett. Chicago: University of Chicago Press, 1996.

PHILOSOPHY ONLINE

American Philosophical Association. The major professional organization for American philosophers, meeting schedules, e-mail addresses for philosophers, university homepages, and more: **http://www.apa.udel.edu/apa/index.html**

Ask Philosophers. Amherst College's website "puts the talents and knowledge of philosophers at the service of the general public" by inviting questions that members of a panel of philosophers answer: **http://www.amherst.edu/askphilosophers**

Episteme Links. This commercial website provides links to electronic texts, journals, papers, philosophers, pictures of philosophers, and a humor section: **http://www.epistemelinks.com**

Ethics Updates. Professor Lawrence M. Hinman's website provides useful ethics information: **http://ethics.sandiego.edu**

Guide to Philosophy on the Internet. Earlham College philosophy professor Peter Stuber's online guide includes links to teaching and learning sites, dictionaries, e-texts, and quotations: **http://www.earlham.edu/~peters/philinks.htm**

Hippias. Hippias searches across eight peer-reviewed metasites. This is a great place to begin searching for philosophy-related information: **http://people.brandeis.edu/~teuber/hippias.html**

The Internet Encyclopedia of Philosophy. Here's an interesting site for very basic research. It's limited but relatively easy to use: **http://www.iep.utm.edu**

The Philosophers Magazine. Just what it sounds like: **http://www.philosophersnet.com**

Philosophy around the Web. Oxford University lecturer Peter J. King's web portal contains links to individual philosophers, diverse areas of philosophy, and a plethora of journals. Find this great online resource at: **http://users.ox.ac.uk/~worc0337/phil_index.html**

Philosophy Documentation Center. This electronic archive and publishing house includes links to all sorts of philosophy sites, and a mail-order supplier of philosophy books: **http://www.pdcnet.org**

Philosophy Now. Another philosophy magazine: **http://www.philosophynow.org**

Stanford Encyclopedia of Philosophy. Accessible articles written by experts: **http://plato.stanford.edu/contents.html**

Wadsworth.com. Nifty website with all sorts of information about Wadsworth philosophy publications (as you might expect) and much more: **http://www.thomsonedu.com/philosophy**

Zeno's Coffeehouse. If you like puzzles, this is the site for you: **http://www.ronbarnette.com/Zeno/zeno.html**

ONLINE STUDY SKILLS AND RESOURCES

Check out these generous sites for reference materials and info about time management, study skills, test taking, and just generally becoming a better student.

Academictips.org. A handy stop for basic tips and info about many of the topics covered in *How to Get the Most Out of Philosophy.* If you want a refresher while you're working online or a different approach, check out: **http://www.academictips.org**

Bartleby.com. A user-friendly portal to reference sources that includes William Strunk Jr.'s *Elements of Style,* the *Columbia Encyclopedia,* the *Encyclopedia of World History,* the *American Heritage Dictionary, Roget's Thesaurus,* and my favorite, the Harvard Classics—the famous "Five-Foot Shelf of Books": **http://www.bartleby.com**

How-to-Study.com. Something for students of all grade levels, including the PQR reading strategy: **http://www.how-to-study.com**

Merriam-Webster OnLine. For fun, this site includes *Word of the Day* and *Word Games* pages, and, for more serious enterprises, the *College Dictionary, College Thesaurus:* **http://www.m-w.com**